PURSUING THE DREAM

MILESTONES IN BLACK AMERICAN HISTORY

PURSUING THE DREAM

FROM THE SELMA–
MONTGOMERY MARCH
TO THE FORMATION OF PUSH (1965–1971)

Sean Dolan

CHELSEA HOUSE PUBLISHERS
New York   Philadelphia

FRONTISPIECE Defying both an ominous sky and militant white supremacists, civil rights demonstrators proudly march from Selma, Alabama, to Montgomery.

ON THE COVER Martin Luther King, Jr., and an army of protesters near the end of the Selma-to-Montgomery march.

Chelsea House Publishers
Editorial Director Richard Rennert
Executive Managing Editor Karyn Gullen Browne
Copy Chief Robin James
Picture Editor Adrian G. Allen
Art Director Robert Mitchell
Manufacturing Director Gerald Levine
Assistant Art Director Joan Ferrigno

Milestones in Black American History
Senior Editor Marian W. Taylor
Series Originator and Adviser Benjamin I. Cohen
Series Consultants Clayborne Carson, Darlene Clark Hine
Series Designer Rae Grant

Staff for PURSUING THE DREAM
Editorial Assistant Sydra Mallery
Picture Researcher Pat Burns

Copyright © 1995 by Chelsea House Publishers, a division of Main Line Book Co. All rights reserved. Printed and bound in the United States of America.

First Printing

1 3 5 7 9 8 6 4 2

Library of Congress Cataloging-in-Publication Data

Dolan, Sean.
   Pursuing the dream 1965–1971: from the Selma – Montgomery march to the for-
mation of PUSH/Sean Dolan
      p. cm. — (Milestones in Black American history)
   Includes bibliographical references and index.
      ISBN 0-7910-2254-4
      ISBN 0-7910-2680-9 (pbk.)
   1. Afro-Americans—Civil Rights—Juvenile literature. 2.Civil rights movements—
United States—History—20th century—Juvenile literature. 3.Southern States—
Race relations—Juvenile literature. [1. Afro-Americans—Civil rights. 2.Civil rights
movements. 3.Southern States—Race relations.] I.Title. II.Series.
E185.615.D64 1995   94–21106
323.1'196073—dc20   CIP
                                                                     AC

CONTENTS

	Introduction	7
	Milestones: 1965–1971	9
1	This Is Selma, Alabama	13
2	How Long?	43
3	The Long, Hot Summers	59
4	Respect	85
5	A Dream Deferred	105
6	Keeping Hope Alive	121
	Further Reading	140
	Index	141

MILESTONES IN BLACK AMERICAN HISTORY

ANCIENT EGYPT, ETHIOPIA, AND NUBIA

THE WEST AFRICAN KINGDOMS (750–1900)

THE AGE OF DISCOVERY AND THE SLAVE TRADE

FROM THE ARRIVAL OF THE ENSLAVED AFRICANS
TO THE END OF THE AMERICAN REVOLUTION (1619–1784)

FROM THE FRAMING OF THE CONSTITUTION
TO *WALKER'S APPEAL* (1787–1829)

FROM THE NAT TURNER REVOLT
TO THE FUGITIVE SLAVE LAW (1831–1850)

FROM *UNCLE TOM'S CABIN*
TO THE ONSET OF THE CIVIL WAR (1851–1861)

FROM THE EMANCIPATION PROCLAMATION
TO THE CIVIL RIGHTS BILL OF 1875 (1863–1875)

FROM THE END OF RECONSTRUCTION
TO THE ATLANTA COMPROMISE (1877–1895)

FROM THE "SEPARATE BUT EQUAL" DOCTRINE
TO THE BIRTH OF THE NAACP (1896–1909)

FROM THE GREAT MIGRATION
TO THE HARLEM RENAISSANCE (1910–1930)

FROM THE SCOTTSBORO CASE
TO THE BREAKING OF BASEBALL'S COLOR BARRIER (1931–1947)

FROM THE DESEGREGATION OF THE ARMED FORCES
TO THE MONTGOMERY BUS BOYCOTT (1948–1956)

FROM THE FOUNDING OF THE SOUTHERN CHRISTIAN
LEADERSHIP CONFERENCE TO THE
ASSASSINATION OF MALCOLM X (1957–1965)

FROM THE SELMA– MONTGOMERY MARCH
TO THE FORMATION OF PUSH (1965–1971)

FROM THE GARY CONVENTION
TO THE PRESENT (1972–)

INTRODUCTION

In the years between the Selma-to-Montgomery march and the formation of People United to Save Humanity (1965 to 1971), the modern civil rights movement reached a turning point. Until then, the movement had concentrated its efforts in the South, on the task of tearing down the barriers of legal segregation that had stood in that region since the end of Reconstruction. Making inspiring use of the philosophy of nonviolent protest, as brilliantly practiced and articulated by the Reverend Martin Luther King, Jr., the movement had succeeded in gaining federal legislation—the 1964 Civil Rights Act—that outlawed segregation in virtually all public institutions.

Despite vocal and often violent opposition in certain parts of the country, particularly the Deep South, the Civil Rights Act reflected a national consensus, almost three and a half centuries after the first black American set foot in the colony of Virginia as a slave, that blacks were entitled to the same legal rights as other Americans. With that principle at last codified in federal law, the focus switched to finding the best way to secure those rights so as to provide blacks, who as a group remained on the bottom rung of the nation's socioeconomic ladder, with genuine equality of opportunity.

In the South, that effort centered on voter registration. For decades, southern whites had used a variety of illegal tactics, including violence, to keep blacks from the polls. Led by King, the Selma-to-Montgomery march was the glorious culmination of the black voter registration effort in the South. But that effort, which resulted directly in the 1965 Voting Rights Act, also revealed with brutal clarity the depth of the racial hatred that existed in the country, as dozens of civil rights activists were murdered and thousands more, including King and the legendary John Lewis, were arrested or brutalized.

The violence with which certain segments of white society resisted the aspirations of black Americans led many younger members of the movement, inspired by such charismatic leaders as Malcolm X and Stokely Carmichael, to question whether nonviolence was still an effective strategy, and integration a worthy goal. In response they offered the rallying cry of "black power," a loosely defined slogan that at least implicitly embraced violence as a possible tactic and rejected white participation in their long struggle.

Meanwhile, for four successive "long, hot summers," the denizens of the black ghettoes of Los Angeles, Newark, and countless other urban centers expressed their rage against a system that excluded them in the form of rioting that constituted the most severe disorder in the country since the Civil War. For northern blacks, the concrete gains of the civil rights movement meant little; longstanding legal guarantees of equal treatment had failed to protect them from the social and economic consequences of a perhaps more subtle but no less pervasive racism than prevailed in the South.

The urban riots culminated in April 1968 following King's assassination by a white gunman. Forever faithful to the redeeming qualities of nonviolence, King had yet grown steadily more radical in his criticism of American society, particularly in its treatment of the poor and its conduct of the war in Vietnam, for which blacks were made to shoulder a disproportionate share of the burden. Though not without his critics, King was the only black leader who could claim a significant degree of allegiance from all segments of black society, the one potentially unifying force in an increasingly fragmented movement. His death, coupled with the increasingly evident white American backlash against the black struggle for social and economic equality, left black Americans, as at so many junctures in their history, with legitimate reason to wonder if this nation was capable of fulfilling its noble promise of liberty and justice for all.

MILESTONES
1965-71

1965
- January: The Reverend Martin Luther King, Jr., chief of the Southern Christian Leadership Conference (SCLC), arrives in Selma, Alabama, to mobilize the registration of black voters.

- February 1–5: Successive civil rights marches, organized by both SCLC and the Student Nonviolent Coordinating Committee (SNCC), result in the arrest of 3,000 black Americans, many of them children.

- March 7 ("Bloody Sunday"): Six hundred blacks attempt a peaceful protest march from Selma to the state capital, Montgomery; attacking the marchers with clubs and tear gas, police and state troopers injure 70 people, some seriously.

- March 9 ("Turnaround Tuesday"): Two thousand protesters, black and white, begin a second Selma-to-Montgomery march. After negotiations with local and state officials, King leads the procession back to Selma.

- March 21: The start of the third Selma-to-Montgomery march opens with 3,200 participants.

- March 25: Led by King, marchers—now 25,000 strong—enter Montgomery.

- August: Congress passes the Voting Rights Act of 1965: the law permits the federal government to supervise local elections where discrimination had been practiced.

- August: The arrest for drunk driving of a young black man in Watts, a Los Angeles ghetto, leads to a six-day riot that takes 14,000 national guardsmen and several thousand policemen to quell. The violence costs 34 lives, injures thousands, and causes $45 million worth of damaged property. It also sparks four subsequent "long hot summers," in which racial violence rends 150 American cities, including Newark, New Jersey; Chicago, Illinois; and Detroit, Michigan.

1966
- SNCC, SCLC, and the Congress of Racial Equality (CORE) unite in a

"March Against Fear," walking from Memphis, Tennessee, to Jackson, Mississippi. The march continues one begun by James Meredith, the first black student at the University of Mississippi, who had fallen to a sniper's bullet earlier in the year. During the March Against Fear, SNCC leader Stokely Carmichael introduces a new slogan: "Black Power."

- "Star Trek" features television's first interracial kiss.

- SNCC officially condemns U.S. involvement in Vietnam. Conservative civil rights groups, such as the National Association for the Advancement of Colored People (NAACP) and the Urban League, criticize SNCC and SCLC for their antiwar stance.

- The Black Panther Party, which advocates armed self-defense against white oppression, is formed to counter the NAACP and other nonviolent civil rights groups.

1967

- January: Singer Aretha Franklin records "Respect," which becomes the unofficial anthem of the civil rights movement. Other great black musicians of the time include jazz pianists Thelonious Monk and Ray Charles, bassist Charles Mingus, saxophonists Ornette Coleman and John Coltrane, and guitarist Wes Montgomery, along with such rockers as Jimi Hendrix, Little Richard, Fats Domino, and Chuck Berry.

- April: Martin Luther King, Jr., denounces U.S. involvement in Vietnam, thereby losing the support of the government and his more conservative followers.

- June: Protesting the Vietnam War, world heavyweight champion Muhammad Ali refuses induction into the army; he is charged with a felony and stripped of his title. (In 1971, the United States Supreme Court would overturn his conviction because of the government's failure to grant him conscientious objector status.)

1968

- April 4: Martin Luther King, Jr., is shot and killed by drifter James Earl Ray in Memphis, Tennessee. During the following week, 130 cities experience unprecedented racial violence.

- November: Carl Stokes is elected mayor of Cleveland, Ohio, becoming the nation's first black chief of a major city.

- June: Several thousand participants in a massive "Poor People's March," organized by King's SCLC successor, Ralph Abernathy, establish "Resurrection City" on the Washington, D.C., mall; the encampment, unofficially governed by a former King aide, the Reverend Jesse Jackson, is destroyed by police.

- October: At the summer Olympic Games, held in Mexico City, sprinters Tommie Smith and John Carlos, respectively the winners of gold and bronze medals for the 200-meter run, raise their black-gloved fists during the "Star-Spangled Banner" to symbolize black power. Both men are stripped of their medals by the U.S. Olympic Committee.

1971

- December: Jesse Jackson vows to continue the fight for civil rights and begins his crusade with the formation of People United to Save Humanity (PUSH).

1

THIS IS SELMA, ALABAMA

THE marchers came east down Broad Street. Near noon on Tuesday, March 9, 1965, those at the head of the orderly procession of 2,000 people reached the crest of the steeply sloped bridge that would carry them over the Alabama River and toward the capital city of Montgomery, 54 miles distant. From the bridge, the marchers saw what awaited them on the other side, where Highway 80 resumed its eastward reach. It was much the same ominous sight that had greeted a smaller group of marchers, some 600 men and women, all of them black, two days earlier.

On both sides of the highway, in front of the hamburger stands and automobile dealerships, stood the checkered vehicles of the Alabama state police. Amost exactly 100 years after the end of the Civil War each car was emblazoned with the flag of the Confederacy, emblem of the rebellious South's defiance of federal law and lingering embrace of white supremacy.

Streaming across the Edmund Pettus Bridge, 2,000 civil rights marchers leave Selma, Alabama, on March 9, 1965. Two days earlier, state troopers had used clubs, truncheons, and tear gas to halt a similar procession.

13

Dressed in blue, the state troopers stood shoulder to shoulder, several rows deep, across the four lanes of Highway 80. Their guns were holstered, but they nervously and eagerly fingered blackjacks and truncheons. Heavy gas masks beneath their blue helmets gave them anonymity and a vaguely satanic air.

On the troopers' flanks were assembled Sheriff Jim Clark's "possemen," a deputized battalion of white citizens that the sheriff led into action wherever it seemed to him Alabama's black populace was threatening the established social order. All the possemen were armed. Some rode horses and carried bullwhips, and others clutched homemade weapons of their own devising: lengths of rubber tubing wrapped with barbed wire. Behind them, farther back from the highway, stood about 100 white spectators, men, women, and children come out to watch the confrontation. A handful of journalists and television cameramen huddled in the shadow of one of the automobile dealerships.

As they had on Sunday, the marchers advanced until they were within a short distance of the blue-clad human barrier stretched out in front of them across Highway 80. On that earlier day, at the last minute a car had pulled up behind the front lines as the procession advanced. It discharged Sheriff Clark and Colonel Al Lingo, commander of the state police. For the sabbath, the towering Clark was dressed in a business suit rather than his usual gold-braid-trimmed uniform with the lapel button that announced his succinct, unyielding motto, NEVER. The word was Clark's response to those who—like the black men and women coming across the Edmund Pettus Bridge toward him from the small city of Selma—were seeking an end to the South's system of legal segregation. In a short time Clark was seen pacing among the troopers and his possemen, his hands wrapped around a tear gas canister. Nearby, Clark's nominal superior,

Selma's director of public safety, Wilson Baker, eyed him nervously.

As they drew near the phalanx of lawmen that Sunday, the two black men at the head of the column, John Lewis of the Student Nonviolent Coordinating Committee (SNCC) and the Reverend Hosea Williams of the Southern Christian Leadership Conference (SCLC), indulged in a brief conversation. "John, can you swim?" Williams asked. "No," answered Lewis,

John Lewis, chairman of the Student Nonviolent Coordinating Committee (SNCC) from 1963 to 1966, heads for jail after a 1964 civil rights protest in Nashville, Tennessee. By the time he took part in the Selma–Montgomery march, the 25-year-old Lewis had already organized scores of sit-ins, helped manage the "Freedom Rides" of 1961, and submitted to countless arrests.

the SNCC chairman. At the age of 25 a legendary veteran—he had been jailed more than 40 times—of the black protest movement in the South, Lewis was "the perfect embodiment," according to historian Robert Weisbrot, "of SNCC's original devotion to religious nonviolence and interracial coalition." Despite the considerable tension that existed between the two organizations the men represented, Williams empathized with Lewis. "I can't either," he said, "and I'm sure we're going to wind up in that river."

Lewis "was the most courageous person that I have ever worked with in the movement," said one colleague. "John would not just follow you into the lion's den, he would lead you into it." Even so, the light-hearted tone of the exchange between the two men could not conceal a very real and well-founded fear. Lewis, Williams, and their respective organizations were resolutely committed to nonviolence in their protest against racial injustice. At other recent civil rights campaigns in the South, however, they had become painfully aware that their commitment was no protection against economic reprisals, imprisonment, physical injury, and even death at the hands of the outraged defenders of white supremacy. Even without the men's past experience, Selma alone had been enough to instill fear in them and their followers, some of them veterans, others neophytes inspired by the steadily escalating momentum of the cause.

SNCC (pronounced "snick" by those in the movement) had been in Selma since 1963, trying to organize the city's 15,000 blacks of voting age to register to vote. The student activists who made up the organization's rank and file had, however, made extremely limited headway. Then the civil rights movement succeeded in focusing national attention on the injustice of legalized segregation in the South. Solidly reflecting that success was President Lyndon Johnson's signing into law, on July 2, the Civil Rights Act of 1964. The legislation, which outlawed segregation in public facilities and discrimination in employment, also empowered the federal government to act forcefully against school segregation. At this point voting rights came to the forefront of the black protest movement in the South.

Despite their frequent disagreements on tactics, both SNCC and SCLC, the two most important civil rights organizations in the South, agreed on one all-important point: that obtaining the right to vote for blacks was necessary to the securing of gains already made by the movement. The two organizations also agreed that the vote was the first step toward attaining real political and economic power for blacks.

Legally, both the U.S. Constitution's 15th Amendment (ratified in 1870) and the 1957 Civil Rights Act guaranteed blacks the right to vote. But for decades, whites in the South had used a combination of intimidation and fraud to prevent blacks from casting their ballots, thereby perpetuating the white stranglehold on political and economic power. As legal segregation came to an end, blacks and whites in the South were quick to recognize the critical importance of the voting-rights issue. In the city of Selma and many other regions of the South, blacks constituted a potential voting majority, which meant they could use the ballot as a democratic means to take and exercise political control. Whites, of course, saw the other side of the coin: to them, the prospect of widespread black exercise of the ballot constituted the most threatening challenge yet to their dominance.

SNCC's activists, who had begun their southern campaign in 1960, had witnessed the full variety of tactics—some of them truly elaborate—employed by

Bearing a simple but blood-chilling message—"This nigger voted"—an effigy hangs from a streetlight in Miami, Florida. Determined to keep blacks from voting, southern racists used every weapon they could think of: literacy tests, poll taxes, economic pressure, and sheer terrorism.

southern whites to keep blacks from voting. Voting registries were opened only at odd and extremely limited times—for one varying two-hour period once or twice a month, for example. Seldom announced in advance, the registration hours were invariably set in the middle of a working day, a time when blacks would find it difficult to leave their jobs.

White voters were generally asked to do nothing more than read a line of the Constitution aloud and sign their names. Blacks who managed to gain access to the registration books were subjected to a literacy test—20 or more questions that required a fairly sophisticated knowledge of the Constitution, U.S. history, and American law. In Alabama, for example, blacks were asked to "understand and explain any article of the Constitution of the United States to the satisfaction of the registrars"—who were, of course, always white and sometimes illiterate. In Selma, prospective black voters were asked, "What two rights does a person have after being charged by a grand jury?" Blacks were disqualified for failing to cross a *t* or dot an *i* on registration forms.

Those very few blacks whom the registrars deemed qualified to vote were required to pay a poll tax before they could actually register. In many jurisdictions, the amount of this tax for one year—not insignificant in itself—was multiplied by the number of years that had passed since the prospective voter had first been eligible to register. For example, a 38-year-old black would-be voter, inspired by a young SNCC field worker to register and somehow succeeding in his attempt, would be required to pay 17 years' worth of poll taxes before he could actually cast a ballot. (This was the amount of time elapsed since he first, at attaining majority at the age of 21, became eligible to vote.) Needless to say, the accumulated cost was often prohibitive for blacks, most of whom occupied the lowest rungs of the South's economic ladder.

When these fraudulent—but under the southern judicial system, legally acceptable—tactics failed to keep blacks from the ballot box, whites used economic coercion. This strategy was especially effective in rural areas, where white control of the land and businesses made black farmers especially vulnerable to such retaliation. Blacks in southwest Tennessee's rural Haywood and Fayette counties, for example, had learned about such tactics in the late 1950s when, motivated by the civil rights movement, they began attempting to register to vote in large numbers.

In *Freedom Bound: A History of America's Civil Rights Movement,* Robert Weisbrot describes the devastating white response in Tennessee: the black activist who led the registration efforts in Fayette County was first denied the annual bank loan that every farmer counts on for seed and equipment; next, the gas company seized his storage tanks, so that he could not operate his tractor; finally, his wife and many other black employees were fired from their jobs in the cafeteria of a white public school. A Fayette County woman who had succeeded in registering suddenly found that the local pharmacist would not dispense medicine for her sick child, the local store would not sell food to her, and no merchant would sell her clothing.

In other instances, black Fayette County businessmen, such as a grocery store proprietor in the town of Brownsville, discovered that white suppliers were no longer willing to do business with them. Thousands of blacks were evicted from their rented spreads on white-owned land and forced to live in tents; trucks delivering food and merchandise for black consumption were turned back at police roadblocks.

The situation in Tennessee ultimately worsened to the extent that 14,000 blacks in the two counties were faced with imminent starvation. At that point, the administration of the newly elected president, John F. Kennedy, intervened by ordering the Department of Agriculture to deliver relief food supplies. Similar instances of economic blackmail took place in the South wherever and whenever blacks threatened to work together to change the prevailing social, political, and economic order. Even more frequently, of course, just the implicit threat of such action was enough to discourage most potential black voters.

Beyond legal obstruction and economic coercion stood the omnipresent threat of physical violence,

Emmett Till, a friendly, outgoing 14-year-old from Chicago, paid with his life for saying "bye, baby" to a white Mississippi woman in 1955. The boy's murderers later bragged about their crime, but a white jury found them innocent anyway.

which had underlain the South's system of white supremacy since the days of slavery.

After the modern civil rights movement was born—with the successful boycott of the segregated bus lines of Montgomery by that city's black populace in 1955–56—the movement's leaders and participants had lived every day with the prospect of violent reprisals.

The movement's most well-known and charismatic leader, the Reverend Martin Luther King, Jr., head of the SCLC, had several times been attacked while speaking. He had once been stabbed in the chest—the blade of the weapon missing his aorta by less than an inch—and his home, like those of many other black activists, had been firebombed. King had first come to national prominence as the leader of the Montgomery boycott; since that inspirational time, scarcely a day had gone by in which his life was not threatened. The firebombings of black churches and homes in the South had become commonplace, and in rural areas especially, many less prominent participants in the movement had been martyred for such transgressions as attempting to register to vote.

Nowhere was white resistance to the black freedom movement more unyielding than in Mississippi, the state with the highest percentage of blacks among its populace. It was in the Magnolia State that SNCC, at the encouragement of a young, exceptionally dedicated, small, shy, soft-spoken, Harlem-born former high-school teacher and Harvard graduate student named Bob Moses, had begun voter registration efforts in 1961. By that time, Mississippi's legacy of racial violence and lawlessness had already made the state notorious.

In August 1955, just four months before the beginning of the Montgomery bus boycott, white men had kidnapped 14-year-old Emmett Till at gunpoint from the home of his great-uncle, Mose Wright, in tiny Money, Mississippi. Till, who hailed from the northern city of Chicago, was visiting his great-uncle with his cousin, but he made a mistake: on one of his first days in Money, Till said "bye, baby" to a white woman in a general store. Three days after his disappearance, authorities hauled his mutilated and beaten body from the Tallahatchee River. There was a bullet wound in his head and a gaping hole where an eye had been; tied to his neck with barbed wire was a cotton-gin fan, which had been used as a weight to sink his corpse in the river's muddy waters.

Two whites, Roy Bryant and J. W. Milam, were arrested and tried for Emmett Till's murder. "I am sure that every last Anglo-Saxon one of you has the courage to acquit these men," the defendant's attorney, John Whitten, told the jury. Although the 64-year-old Mose Wright took the witness stand to identify the men who had abducted Till—an unimaginably brave act for a black man in that day's Mississippi—an all-white jury found them innocent. Whitten later admitted to *Life* magazine correspondent William Bradford Huie that he had never even bothered to ask his clients if they had committed the gruesome crime. When Huie did ask them, Bryant and Milam confessed with little prodding; Milam, in fact, said he considered the killing simply part of a "war"—a conflict that he said had started in 1954, when a U.S. Supreme Court decision outlawed segregation in public education.

(That decision, in the case of *Brown v. Board of Education of Topeka, Kansas*, had inspired blacks, as in Montgomery the following year, to begin organized protests of the continued denial of their full constitutional rights. The court's ruling on education had terrified southern whites, who recognized that it threatened, by extension, the entire framework of legal segregation.)

Perhaps because there was a child involved, the Till case attracted national publicity, but it hardly represented the first shot in the "war" that Milam had spoken of. In the Mississippi Delta region of the state, where the Till lynching had taken place, blacks outnumbered whites by four to one in some counties, and the political status quo was defended as unrelentingly as the "honor" of white women. In some of the Mississippi regions where blacks constituted an outright majority, the voter registration rolls held the names of no black citizens at all, and the white beneficiaries of this inequity intended to keep it that way.

Three months before Till's arrival, the Reverend George Lee, the first black to register to vote in Humphreys County, had been shotgunned to death in the Delta town of Belzoni. The sheriff suggested that the buckshot pellets found in Lee's mouth were fillings from his teeth, and the authorities officially ruled the death a traffic accident. Another would-be black voter, Belzoni grocer Gus Courts, stubbornly kept his name on the registration rolls despite numerous death threats and a tripling of the monthly rent for his store. He, too, was shot; although he survived, he left the state. The pattern of violence and economic retaliation persuaded all but three of the 400 Belzoni blacks who had registered to withdraw their names from the rolls. In Brookhaven, further south in the Delta, Lamar Smith was murdered in the blinding light of high noon on the steps of the courthouse; his crime: having voted in the state's Democratic party primary. No one was ever arrested for the shooting.

Andrew Young of SCLC, Martin Luther King's most trusted aide, attempted to dissuade SNCC workers from their efforts in Mississippi. He warned them that conditions there were simply too dangerous, but SNCC's reputation for fearlessness was well earned, and despite threats, arrests, beatings, and jail sentences, they persisted. "Bob Moses was a little bitty fella," remembered Unita Blackwell, a black resident of Sunflower County who saw him in action. (Blackwell's recollection is quoted in *Voices of Freedom*, an oral history of the civil rights movement compiled by Henry Hampton and Steve Fayer.) "And he stood up to this sheriff and Bob said, 'I'm from SNCC.' I had never saw that before. From that day on, I said, 'Well, I can stand myself.' People remember them people. SNCC went where nobody went. They was about the nuttiest ones they was. Ended up in some of the most isolated places and drug people out of there to vote."

SNCC had by now been joined in its voter registration efforts by SCLC and two northern-based civil rights organizations, the Congress of Racial Equality (CORE) and the National Association for the Advancement of Colored People (NAACP). White Mis-

sissippians responded to these "agitators" predictably. In February 1963, a car in which Moses was traveling with two colleagues near Greenwood was raked by 13 shots from a .45, leaving the driver, Jimmy Travis, seriously wounded in the neck.

Four months later, on June 11, 1963, President Kennedy gave a nationwide address in which he characterized civil rights as a "moral issue." Calling that issue "as clear as the American Constitution," Kennedy committed himself to the passage of legislation that would demonstrate the "proposition that race has no place in American life or law." Mississippi showed its opinion of the president's words on the very night of the speech. In Jackson, the state capital, a white man hid near the driveway of 37-year-old Medgar Evers, longtime field secretary for the NAACP's Mis-

Civil rights pioneer Medgar Evers, Mississippi's innovative NAACP field secretary, was assassinated outside his Jackson home in 1963. The killer, White Citizens Council member Byron de la Beckwith, escaped justice for three decades, but in early 1994, a mixed-race jury found him guilty of the murder and sent him to prison for life.

sissippi branch. As Evers approached his house, the
man raised his high-powered rifle, fired a single shot,
and killed him.

The youthful adherents of SNCC and SCLC regarded the NAACP, the oldest and most prestigious
of the nation's civil rights organizations, as hopelessly
conservative. Evers, however, had been shaking
things in his NAACP jurisdiction. Energized by the
youthful idealism of the SNCC activists, he had been
leading a black boycott of Jackson's white-owned
businesses, a move that apparently earned him the
murderous enmity of certain local whites. A fingerprint on the weapon that killed Evers linked it to
Byron de la Beckwith, a prominent member of the
local White Citizens Council (WCC). (A white-
supremacist group with chapters throughout the
South, the WCC had been organized after the *Brown*
decision.)

Despite the fingerprint, the all-white juries in two
trials failed to convict Beckwith. The suitability of
prospective jurors in those cases was determined by,
among other things, their response to this question:
"Do you believe it's illegal to kill a nigger in the state
of Mississippi?" At the first trial, jurors saw Mississippi
governor Ross Barnett, who owed his election to high
office to the support of the WCC, shaking Beckwith's
hand. At liberty for almost 30 years, Beckwith would
be tried again in 1993. Early the following year, a
jury—this time containing blacks as well as whites—
found him guilty of the murder of Medgar Evers.

By the end of the summer of 1964, civil rights
workers in Mississippi had been arrested 1,000 times,
shot at 35 times, and beaten 80 times. Thirty homes,
churches, and buildings had been bombed, and three
other civil rights workers had been killed. In Selma,
blacks working to gain the ballot experienced the full
force of such tactics. When Bernard Lafayette and
other members of SNCC began their voter registra-

tion work in Selma in 1963, only 335 of the city's 15,000 eligible black voters (out of a total city population of 29,000) were registered. After 32 black teachers attempted to register to vote, they were fired. John Lewis was arrested for leading a peaceful demonstration at the Dallas County Courthouse; a SNCC colleague was brutally beaten while in police custody. When SNCC's overall-clad, pipe-smoking executive secretary, James Forman, convened a "mass meeting" at the Tabernacle Baptist Church to impress the importance of the vote upon justifiably fearful local blacks, a mob of several hundred of Clark's possemen, armed with clubs, whips, and cattle prods, menaced the gathering.

On October 7, 1963, which SNCC had declared "Freedom Day," 350 blacks gathered at the courthouse to register. Under a hot sun and the watchful eyes of FBI agents, Department of Justice officials, reporters, and several celebrities—including an increasingly furious James Baldwin, the nation's foremost black writer—the would-be voters were subjected to various indignities and injustices. Sheriff Clark, dressed in his gold-braid-trimmed uniform with a huge silver star pinned over his breast pocket and a thick black gun-belt buckled under his protruding paunch, personally drove blacks from the steps of the courthouse with his swagger stick. White onlookers cheered.

Those who resisted were arrested, as were those who attempted to bring food and water to the people on line. Inside, the registrars did everything within their power to ensure that the line moved slowly. At the end of the day only a small number of blacks—50, according to the *New York Times*; 20, according to Baldwin; 5, according to John Lewis—had succeeded in registering.

In the fall of 1964, Selma activists, chief among them Amelia Boynton, invited Martin Luther King, Jr., and SCLC to visit the community. Neither the

white authorities in Selma nor the members of SNCC
were entirely pleased by the invitation. To most
blacks and whites, King was the very embodiment of
the civil rights struggle. In December 1964, he had
become, at just 35 years of age, the youngest recipient
ever of the Nobel Peace Prize, and his incomparably
eloquent explications of the power of nonviolent protest had given the movement much of its moral force.
His presence in Selma therefore virtually guaranteed
that the struggle in the city would become the focus
of national and even worldwide attention. This, for
different reasons, troubled both SNCC and their segregationist opponents.

Though SNCC had been founded, in large part,
by students inspired by King's example, most of whom
still shared his commitment to nonviolence, a rift
between the two organizations had been growing since
the younger group's beginnings in 1960. To a great
extent, the differences were a matter of approach.
Because of King's fame and the media attention he
could command, SCLC had adopted a strategy of
organizing large-scale nonviolent protests, tied to a
specific local issue—for example, desegregation of
lunch counters and department stores. These protests
were intended to attract national attention and action
through the intervention of the news media and, it
was hoped, the broad-based public sympathy that
would result from such coverage.

SCLC denied that it wanted to provoke a violent
reaction to their protests, but its members counted on
the angry response of local white authorities; disproportionate violence would arouse the nation's conscience and prod the otherwise slow-moving federal
government into action. For eight decades, for example, the nation had tolerated the evils of segregation,
but the sight of Birmingham, Alabama, sheriff "Bull"
Connor's men turning high-pressure fire hoses and
police dogs on protesting schoolchildren had changed

things. Birmingham had sparked not only widespread revulsion and anger but the public support Congress needed to pass the Civil Rights Act of 1964. In Selma, King and SCLC were counting on the notoriously volatile Clark to create a political climate favorable for the passage of a national voting rights act. Such legislation would eliminate literacy tests and poll taxes and allow for federal registrars to come into areas such as Selma and register black voters.

SNCC also supported passage of a federal voting rights act, but its own efforts in Selma, as elsewhere, tended toward long-term grassroots efforts on the local level. SCLC specialized in the orchestration of short-term, high-profile confrontations; SNCC favored teaching poorly educated blacks how to pass the

Interrupting a peaceful 1963 civil rights demonstration in Birmingham, Alabama, firefighters pound teenagers with high-velocity water cannons. Birmingham's violent response to black activists, orchestrated by the city's truculent police chief, "Bull" Connor, aroused national indignation and eventually led to passage of the 1964 Civil Rights Act.

literacy tests, educating them about the importance of the ballot, and developing local coalitions and political organizations. Extremely democratic in its decision making and organization, SNCC tended to be suspicious of the cult of personality that surrounded King, who generally had the final say on all important SCLC matters. "SCLC pushes the idea that local people need leaders like Martin Luther King," said a community activist in Selma, "while SNCC says that local people build their own leaders, out of their own communities."

It was often argued that the movement benefited from both approaches, but SNCC charged that SCLC's methods sometimes undermined local initiative. There was no doubt that for a time King and SCLC could arouse and mobilize the energies of a dormant community. SNCC believed, however, that in SCLC's focus on immediate and tangible victories, it paid too little attention to educating and encouraging local leadership, which could continue the struggle after SCLC left a given locale for the next crisis spot. "For the local leaders" with whom SNCC worked, wrote historian David Garrow in his Pulitzer prizewinning *Bearing the Cross: Martin Luther King and the Southern Christian Leadership Conference,* "the campaign was a way to change Selma, but for King and SCLC it was a way to challenge the entire structure of racial exclusion in Alabama politics and to force [President] Lyndon Johnson's hand on a federal voting statute."

With King's arrival in Selma in January 1965, every member of the SNCC board but one favored a cessation of the organization's own efforts there. That one naysayer was Lewis, whose commitment to non-violent protest and to King was unwavering. (He also served, in fact, on SCLC's board of directors.) Following, according to Weisbrot, the long-standing precept "that no one could tell John Lewis what to do," the board therefore voted to direct SNCC workers to follow their individual conscience about participation in SCLC-led activities.

Selma's white authorities were also divided over tactics, and for them King's coming posed a number of problems. The city's newly elected young mayor, Joseph Smitherman, sometimes described as a "progressive segregationist," wanted to maintain the racial status quo. But he also hoped to pacify black unrest in the city by making minor political concessions, such as paving the roads in the black sections of town. He believed that the way to defuse King's protest in Selma was to meet it with restraint, not with the kind of violence that had taken place in Birmingham. Smitherman knew that to defeat King, he would have to find a way to control Clark, his possemen, and the

Clearly resentful, a room clerk registers the first African American—Martin Luther King, Jr.—ever to stay at Selma's Albert Hotel. Moments after this picture was taken, a white, self-described "Nazi" landed two hard punches on King's temple; the rights leader was stunned but not injured, and his attacker was arrested.

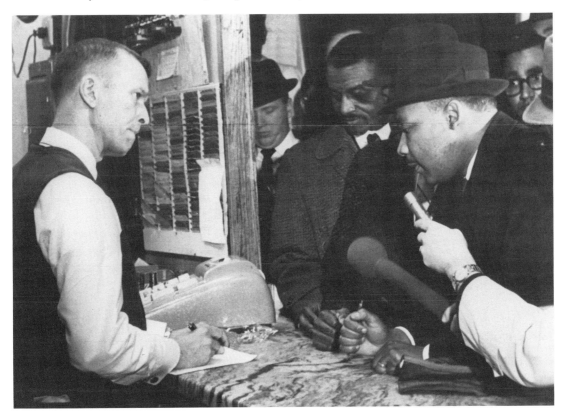

Visiting Selma in February 1965, Martin Luther King, Jr. (third from left), shakes hands with would-be voters. At first, SCLC and SNCC's registration efforts had little impact on Selma: no matter how many black applicants assembled, and no matter how long and patiently they waited, their fierce desire to vote was countered by whites' determination to keep them from the polls.

more volatile elements of the community. To that end the mayor created a new position, director of public safety, with nominal authority over the sheriff. To that job he appointed Wilson Baker, a lawman reputed to be adept in nonviolent enforcement techniques.

On January 18, 1965, King and Lewis spent a frustrating day; not one of 400 assembled blacks succeeded in registering to vote. Then, as King attempted to become the first black to stay at the Albert Hotel, he was attacked by an out-of-town white supremacist who landed two punches to his head. King and his aides, however, were less disturbed by that than they were by Clark's uncharacteristically peaceful behavior that day. His avoidance of confrontation continued Selma's pattern of official restraint, which had prevailed since SCLC had started its activities there three weeks earlier. Media interest in the Selma protest was flagging. Then Mayor Smitherman and Public Safety

Director Baker learned from a white informant within SCLC that the organization's leadership had decided to stage one last march to the courthouse. If nothing occurred to revitalize their campaign, they would move on to other locales.

But if King and his aides had had an informant of their own, they would have learned some electrifying news that night. Clark, in a state of extreme frustration over the course of events thus far, told a horrified Smitherman that the next day he intended to get tough. On January 19, as the television cameras rolled, he resumed driving would-be registrants from the courthouse steps with his billy club. Sixty-seven blacks were arrested for "unlawful assembly," but it was the jailing of Amelia Boynton that made front-page news around the country. When she resisted Clark's order to move off the courthouse sidewalk, he manhandled her and had her taken to jail. The next day, he arrested all 150 blacks who came to the courthouse to register, including Lewis, whom he disparaged as an "agitator . . . the lowest form of humanity." Two days later, 105 black schoolteachers, traditionally among the most respected and conservative members of the black community, marched around the courthouse in silent protest. Clark's possemen drove them away with billy clubs and electric cattle prods.

The unprovoked attack on its educators further galvanized Selma's already aroused black community. According to Andrew Young, the assault on the schoolteachers "was the most significant thing that

*Sheriff Jim Clark shoves
the Reverend C. T. Vivian,
an SCLC official and close aide
of King's, away from the Selma
registrar's office in February
1965. Extensively covered
by the news media, Clark's
brutal tactics defeated his own
purposes by inspiring
nationwide sympathy for
southern blacks.*

[had] happened in the racial movement since Birmingham." The stand taken by their teachers made a huge impression on Selma's students. "What impressed me most about the day that the teachers marched was just the idea of them being there," young Sheyann Webb was quoted as saying in *Voices of Freedom*. "Prior to their marching, I used to have to go to school and it was like a report, you know. I had to report to my teachers, because they were afraid. They were just as afraid as my parents were, because they would lose their jobs. And it was amazing to see how many teachers participated." When asked by her parents what she wanted as a gift for her next birthday, Sheyann said she wanted them to register to vote.

Clark was just hitting his stride. A new group of protesters arrived at the courthouse on January 25, and the sheriff resumed his bullying and the indiscriminate use of his nightstick. When 53-year-old Annie Lee Cooper, a woman of considerable heft, told Clark that neither she nor any of the other protesters was afraid of him, he shoved her; she dropped him with two powerful punches. A trio of deputies then pinioned her to the pavement while Clark sat on her stomach and clubbed her senseless. Photographs of the out-of-control sheriff ran in newspapers around the country.

On February 1, King led a peaceful mass march on the courthouse, where he and 770 demonstrators, many of them schoolchildren, were arrested for violating Selma's parade ordinances. The next day 550

The Reverend Martin Luther King, Jr. (left), prays with the Reverend Ralph Abernathy (center) and an aide after their arrest in Selma. The three men—along with 260 others—were charged with holding an "illegal parade" after they staged a voting-rights march in February 1965.

more nonviolent protesters, again most of them children, were arrested. Three days later, another 500
young demonstrators were incarcerated. By this point,
3,000 blacks were being held in Dallas County jails
for the crime of seeking the right to vote. On February
5, an SCLC advertisement ran in the *New York Times*.
Written in the form of a letter by King from his jail
cell, it concluded with a powerful indictment. "This
is Selma, Alabama," King wrote. "There are more
Negroes in jail with me than there are on the voting
rolls."

> **At this point, the United States was escalat-
> ing its involvement in the war in Vietnam for the
> ostensible purpose of instilling its own values of
> "democracy" in that country. Now here, in the
> nation's most important newspaper, was the im-
> age of the Nobel Peace Prize–winner being held
> in one of America's jails for daring to challenge
> his nation's commitment to its proclaimed ide-
> als—in essence, a political prisoner in a land that
> prided itself on being "the leader of the free
> world."**

Clark, of course, was unmoved. Although SCLC
leaders jokingly suggested making him an honorary
member of the organization in recognition of all the
help he had given their protest—"Every time it ap-
pears that the movement is dying out," said one,
"Sheriff Clark comes to our rescue"—the confrontation was soon to escalate from violent to deadly.
When King was released and went to Washington to
meet with President Johnson, the Reverend James
Bevel of SCLC led a new delegation to the Selma
courthouse. There, an infuriated Clark—"You're
making a mockery out of justice," the lawman
screamed at the minister—clubbed him into submis-

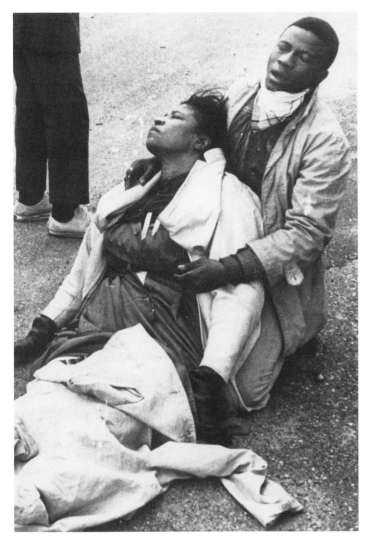

Felled by a blast of tear gas, civil rights activists lie gasping on "Bloody Sunday," March 7, 1965, the first day demonstrators tried to march from Selma to the Alabama state capital at Montgomery. Armed troopers had charged the peaceful protesters, leaving 70 with cracked skulls and other serious injuries.

sion and took him and his allies into custody. Two days later, on February 10, Clark's possemen used electric cattle prods to run 165 young demonstrators several miles outside the city limits. Less than a week later, on February 16, Clark punched the Reverend C. T. Vivian on the steps of the courthouse while the clergyman lectured him on his responsibilities under the Constitution.

By this time, King and the other SCLC leaders were hoping to expand their protest for voter rights into the areas surrounding Selma. They scheduled a nighttime rally for February 18 in the small city of Marion, some 60 miles to the northwest. The demonstrators arrived to find the town "surrounded" (in the words of protester Albert Turner) by state troopers, Clark's possemen, various other law enforcement forces, and "everyone . . . who felt like beating folk up." What followed, according to one Alabama newspaper, was a "nightmare of State Police brutality and stupidity," with policemen and local whites unashamedly attacking marchers and even television journalists and newspapermen who were covering the event. A young black demonstrator, Jimmie Lee Jackson, was shot at point-blank range in the stomach by a state trooper as he came to the aid of his grandfather and mother, who had been beaten senseless.

After a week in the hospital, Jackson died. King preached at his funeral to an estimated 1,000 mourners, and in the aftermath SCLC decided to organize a nonviolent march from Selma to Montgomery, the state capital. The official reason for the march was to petition Alabama's segregationist governor, George Wallace, for protection of registering voters, but the trek would serve several other purposes as well. For King, it was a means to put increased pressure on the federal government for a voting rights act. For James Bevel, it was an opportunity for the movement to heal its wounds by coming together in grief over Jackson's death. He explained his plans by recalling "some of the classical strategies of Gandhi," the Indian leader who used the tactics of nonviolent protest and civil disobedience to free his homeland from British rule.

"When you have a great violation of the people and there's a great sense of injury," said Bevel, "you have to give people an honorable means and context in which to express and eliminate that grief and speak decisively and succinctly back to the issue. Otherwise the movement will break down in violence and

chaos." Most important, the Selma-to-Montgomery march was powerful political symbolism: one month short of the centennial anniversary of the Civil War's end, blacks were marching—nonviolently—on the Cradle of the Confederacy, still in search of perhaps the most fundamental of the democratic rights promised America's citizens under the Constitution.

And so, on the morning of Sunday, March 7, Hosea Williams (in the absence of King, who was preaching at his church in Atlanta) and John Lewis led 600 black protesters from Selma across the Edmund Pettus Bridge to within 50 feet of the battalion of state troopers and possemen that blocked their way to Montgomery. "This is an unlawful assembly," intoned Major John Cloud of the state police, speaking

Alabama troopers attack civil rights marchers—one of whom (in light coat at center) is SNCC leader John Lewis —on Sunday, March 7, 1965. Television film of the violence shocked the nation; "We have witnessed," said a grim Martin Luther King, Jr., "an eruption of the disease of racism which seeks to destroy all America."

through a bullhorn. He directed the marchers to dis-
assemble and return either to their homes or Brown
Chapel, the march's starting point.

"May we have a word with the major?" Williams
asked.

"There is no word to be had," the lawman replied.
Williams repeated his inquiry, to the same response.
"You have two minutes to turn around and go back to
your church," Cloud said. Williams, Lewis, and all
those behind them stood their ground, many with
their heads bowed in silent prayer. After approximately one minute, according to eyewitnesses, Cloud
ordered his men forward. To the cheers of the white
onlookers, the state troopers charged in a great rush,
billy clubs flailing, immediately overrunning the front
ranks of the demonstrators and putting those behind
to flight. The acrid smell of tear gas—Clark, said one
observer, tossed the first canister—soon filled the air,
though its stinging cloud could not veil the carnage.

**Lewis lay felled almost where he had stood,
his skull fractured by a policeman's club. Nearby
lay more wounded, including Amelia Boynton
and four female friends, who had been similarly
handled. Screams and shouts and the thump of
billy clubs hitting their targets filled the air while
Clark's mounted possemen rode down the fleeing
demonstrators. Wilson Baker attempted in vain
to get Clark to restrain his men. "I've already
waited a month too damn long about moving in,"
the sheriff told him. Running for her life ahead
of the horsemen, little Sheyann Webb felt herself
being lifted off her feet and carried in the arms
of Hosea Williams. She ordered him to put her
down because he was not running fast enough.
"And I ran and I ran and I ran," she remembered
25 years later.**

Seventy blacks were treated at area hospitals for injuries sustained during Bloody Sunday, as the day was soon labeled; many more ministered to their own wounds. That night, television networks interrupted their prime-time broadcasts to show film footage of the bloody events in Selma. By Tuesday morning, 50 denunciations of what Senator Jacob Javits of New York called an "exercise in terror" had been given on the floor of the U.S. Senate and the House of Representatives, and editorials castigating Selma for its lawlessness appeared in newspapers around the nation. In response to King's call, hundreds of sympathizers, including 450 white members of various religious orders, descended on Selma to take part in the next march, which was scheduled for Tuesday, March 9.

And so on that morning they came again, 2,000 of them this time, blacks and whites, men and women, children and their elders, over the bridge and toward the forbidden city, led by King this time to within 50 feet of the menacing human barrier that again barred their way. At King's direction, the group knelt in silent prayer, the thoughts of many no doubt distracted from contemplation of the divine by unvoiced speculation about what would happen next. Then, to the amazement of onlookers—maybe King really was "de Lawd," as SNCC staffers sometimes sarcastically referred to him—the wall of police parted, leaving the road to Montgomery free. And King turned the procession around, and led the marchers back into Selma to Brown Chapel.

2

HOW LONG?

THE "Tuesday Turnaround," as SNCC's outraged membership was quick to term the events of March 9, 1965, marked a literal turning point in the civil rights movement. King had been caught between two forces: the momentum of the movement he had helped generate and a temporary injunction prohibiting the march, issued by the usually sympathetic federal judge Frank Johnson. King had envisioned the turnaround as a compromise that would both satisfy the needs of his followers for direct action and comply with the judicial directive. Still placing his hope in a national voting rights act, King was reluctant to antagonize the federal government, especially by disobeying the order of a federal judge. Of the various organs of local, state, and national government, it was the federal courts that had consistently been most sympathetic to the civil rights movement and awarded it its most meaningful legal victories.

Very late on Monday night, explaining to U.S. attorney general Nicholas Katzenbach why he was

Facing a sea of frustrated civil rights activists outside Selma's Brown Chapel, Martin Luther King, Jr., explains the "turnaround" of Tuesday, March 9, 1965. King had agreed to postpone the Selma-to-Montgomery march to prevent bloodshed, but his move infuriated many of the movement's young militants.

43

inclined to go forward with the next day's march, King said, "You have not been a black man in America for 300 years." Nevertheless, he agreed to the compromise solution of a turnaround worked out with federal mediator Leroy Collins, who also obtained Lingo's and Clark's assurances that they would not allow their men to attack the marchers.

But the rank-and-file of the movement in Selma had not been privy to King's deliberations, and they reacted to the turnaround with mixed degrees of confusion, bafflement, loyalty, and outrage. SNCC's members were especially angry. James Forman denounced the turnaround as a "classic example of trickery against the people," and others even accused King of cowardice. Some of the movement's younger members had questioned King's individual bravery after 1961, when he declined to participate personally in the freedom rides (a dangerous campaign against segregated interstate bus transportation, organized by John Lewis and James Farmer of CORE.) Even King's success in ensuring the safety of the marchers on Tuesday was regarded less as a triumph of pragmatic negotiation than as a by-product of circumstances. The police had not attacked, argued Forman in the tumultuous hours at Brown Chapel that followed the turnaround, because the crowd of demonstrators on this day was racially mixed, unlike the crowd of two days earlier, when only blacks had set out for Montgomery. "They don't beat white people," Forman said. "It's Negroes they beat and kill."

Forman's words were by no means universally accepted then or afterward, but they were indicative of the steadily growing differences between SNCC and SCLC. Never again, after Selma, would the two organizations succeed in maintaining more than a facade of unity. Their divergence would reflect American society's difficulties in devising solutions to its racial problems—problems that were, in many regards, much more difficult to articulate and define than the more easily dramatized and clear-cut injustices then facing civil rights workers in the South.

> **Feeding the dissatisfaction of Forman and others was their deepening conviction that nonviolence had just about lost its effectiveness as a strategy. For many of the younger leaders and members of SNCC, it was simply a way to put moral and political pressure on those in power, and it could be traded for more effective methods when necessary. But for men like King, Lewis, and James Lawson (one of the founders of SNCC), nonviolence was a deeply held personal philosophy, a core element of their individual religious beliefs.**

King, for example, preached the Christian necessity of loving one's oppressors. He held out the possibility of transforming one's enemies through the redemptive power of love, and refused to defend himself even when—as happened on several occasions—he was physically attacked. In Selma, when Sheriff Clark was briefly hospitalized with chest pains, 200 of King's young followers knelt in prayer for him outside the courthouse. And when the marchers returned to Brown Chapel from the Edmund Pettus Bridge on Turnaround Tuesday, they sang, "Governor Wallace we love you in our hearts."

But some found it difficult, indeed unnatural, to maintain such charity toward those who were trying to do them harm. Others simply questioned whether, in the wake of such events as "Bloody Sunday," nonviolence alone was sufficient. And most found it enormously stressful to try to live up to the ideals practiced by such men as King and Bob Moses. Har-

Arm-in-arm, protesters brave a line of club-carrying state troopers in Selma. The standoff, which ended in an uneasy truce, was one of many that took place during the tension-packed week after the aborted trek to Montgomery on March 9.

vard psychiatrist Alvin Poussaint examined civil rights workers who had been beaten in the course of protests. "No, I don't hate those white men," they would invariably say to him, "Dr. King says the only way we can win our freedom is through love." Poussaint found that the students' displaced anger inevitably expressed itself in the form of violent verbal and physical encounters with their colleagues.

Stress-related physical ailments were common among civil rights workers in the South, and burnout was frequent. By 1965, even the saintly Bob Moses had had enough, and he took a leave of absence from SNCC and returned to the North. Connie Curry, one of Moses's SNCC colleagues, remembered in 1983 that "we used to have arguments of whether or not nonviolence was a technique or a way of life, and that was probably one of the biggest debates in the early days of SNCC. Because I maintained, as did other people, that nonviolence as a way of life was good as an ideal, but it was something that was absolutely alien to all of our backgrounds and the way that we were raised. . . . That's why being beaten and thrown into jail and trying to love everybody while they did it to you . . . was bound to mess you up. I mean, look what it did to Bob Moses. . . . It broke his heart."

For CORE's Dave Dennis, the virulence of white racism ruled out peaceful opposition. In Mississippi in 1964, Dennis had been asked to give the eulogy for slain freedom worker James Chaney, and he found himself, as he explained in *Voices of Freedom*, simply unable to preach his organization's official stance of nonviolence. To do so, he suddenly decided as he began his speech, was to reside in a "fantasy world," because "this country—you cannot make a man change by speaking a foreign language, he has to understand what you're talking about—this country operates, operated then, and still operates, on violence. I mean, it's an eye for an eye, a tooth for a tooth."

Such sentiments were in evidence at Brown Chapel in the mournful aftermath of Bloody Sunday, recalled Frederick Reese, a local preacher and activist: "There was a great question in the minds of many people whether or not the nonviolent method should really be employed continually in the movement. There was some indication there were those who really wanted to take up whatever arms they had and retaliate with violence." Even Fred Shuttlesworth, a Birmingham minister who had cofounded the SCLC, had begun to question the effectiveness

Former Black Muslim spokesman Malcolm X (right) shares a moment of unity with Martin Luther King, Jr. Although he had launched a barrage of scornful verbal assaults on King, Malcolm offered his cooperation just before his death in early 1965.

of nonviolence. "You can't shame segregation-ists," Shuttlesworth said. "Rattlesnakes don't commit suicide."

By this time, many of the movement's younger participants had come under the powerful influence of Malcolm X, the tall, charismatic former spokesman for the Nation of Islam (often referred to as the Black Muslims). At SNCC's invitation, Malcolm had spoken in Selma on February 4, just two and a half weeks before gunmen affiliated with his former organization shot him dead. Fiercely intelligent, a mesmerizing, combative speaker, Malcolm had educated and rehabilitated himself during the six years he spent in prison between 1946 and 1952. (He was born in Omaha, Nebraska, in 1925.)

After his break with the Nation of Islam, Malcolm had stopped preaching that whites were inherently evil, but he never embraced nonviolence as a strategy. Discussing the situation of black Americans, he used these words: "When a man is on a hot stove, he says, 'I'm coming up. I'm getting up.' Violently or nonviolently doesn't even enter into the picture—'I'm coming up, do you understand?'" At the very least, said Malcolm, blacks should practice militant self-defense, and they should utilize "any means necessary" to gain their freedom. Malcolm believed that American society was racist and that blacks could expect to get from it only what they took themselves. His most influential message—an insistence on black pride and self-reliance—was one that many young blacks took to heart and that the more militant members of SNCC believed had been betrayed by the movement's strategy.

Malcolm's criticisms of King hit home with many of these disillusioned young blacks. Eager for results, they had grown frustrated with their leadership; they saw the Tuesday Turnaround, for example, as the result of King's misplaced trust in the federal government's good will. On the 1963 March on Washington, the largest civil rights protest in the nation's history and the site of King's famous "I Have a Dream" speech, Malcolm had only scornful remarks. "Who ever heard of angry revolutionists swinging their bare feet together with their oppressor in lily-pad park pools, with gospels and guitars and 'I Have a Dream' speeches?" he asked. "The black masses in America were—and still are—having a nightmare." He was equally scathing about King's Nobel Peace Prize. "He got the peace prize, we got the problem," Malcolm said. "If I'm following a general, and he's leading me into battle,

and the enemy tends to give him rewards, or awards,
I get suspicious of him. Especially if he gets a peace
award before the war is over."

Malcolm's militant rhetoric hid a certain respect for King and his work. At the conclusion
of his trip to Selma, he spoke to Coretta Scott
King about her husband. "Mrs. King, will you
tell Dr. King that I'm sorry I won't get to see
him?" he said. "I want him to know that I didn't
come to make his job more difficult. I thought
that if the white people understood what the
alternative was they would be willing to listen to
Dr. King." Like Malcolm, the movement's more
restive elements maintained an abiding admira-
tion for King, despite disagreements over strategy. Indeed, there was no denying his stature,
and no other black leader could command such a
broad audience.

Those who listened intently to King ranged from
President Lyndon Johnson—who on March 14 called
King in Selma, inviting him to come to the nation's
capitol the next day to attend his nationally televised
speech on the Selma crisis—to the poor black share-
croppers whom SNCC volunteers attempted to organize in the southern countryside. In such regions,
Stokely Carmichael explained in Clayborne Carson's
history of SNCC, *In Struggle*, the organization found
it prudent to ignore its differences with King: "People
loved King. . . . I've seen people in the South climb
over each other just to say, 'I touched him! I touched
him!' . . . I'm even talking about the young. The old
people had more love and respect. They even saw him
like a God. These were the people we were working
with and I had to follow in his footsteps when I went
in there. The people didn't know what was SNCC.

They just said, 'You one of Dr. King's men?' 'Yes, Ma'am, I am.'"

By birth a member of elite black southern society, King was well educated, intellectual, sometimes remote in person. Yet in his preaching he was able to speak to all. The Reverend James Smith, a black minister from Memphis, Tennessee, heard him preach there in 1968. "There was something about Dr. King," said Smith. "A man who could walk with kings but he was just as simple when he spoke that all of us understood him. Never met a man like that before." The oft-critical Carmichael cited King's "love for the people" and his "honesty" as the reasons for his own "love and respect" for King. Carmichael marveled at King's ability to articulate complex political, philosophical, and moral concepts in a way his listeners could understand and respond to. "The response was like a shepherd leading his flock, going to give them water on green pastures," he said. "They responded. You know, I'm often amazed. People say, 'You know, Dr. King, he speaks with such big words that poor people can't understand.' No, King was a true teacher. I mean, he would teach. He would speak. Use all those broad concepts, but they would understand exactly what he was saying."

On March 15, President Johnson addressed the nation. His speech covered a number of points: he pledged his administration's unequivocal support for a national voting rights act; stated that it was "deadly wrong to deny any of your fellow Americans the right to vote in this country"; praised the demonstrators in Selma, who had, he said, "awakened the conscience of this nation"; compared the events in Selma to those of Lexington and Concord (where the first shots of the American Revolution were fired) and Appomattox (scene of the Confederate surrender that ended the Civil War) in their historical significance. Johnson concluded by invoking the anthem of the movement, "We Shall Overcome."

Nonviolence would always remain the corner-stone of King's philosophy—he would practice it, he often said, even if he were the only person in America to do so—but his ideas were evolving. According to John Lewis and C. T. Vivian, Johnson's speech brought a tear to King's eye, but even so, he harbored fewer illusions about the federal government than his critics might have supposed. He had, in the weeks preceding the Selma campaign, been hounded nearly to despair by the Federal Bureau of Investigation (FBI). In an attempt to discredit him and destroy his movement, the bureau had been engaged in an ongoing program of harassment of him, including covert surveillance, wiretapping, and bugging. The director of the FBI, J. Edgar Hoover, had characterized King to journalists as the "most notorious liar" in America and "one of the lowest characters in the country." And Hoover's operatives had attempted to blackmail King into relinquishing leadership of the movement by threatening to make public evidence of his alleged extramarital sexual activity. An even better alternative for King, the FBI suggested, was to commit suicide.

Although, for the time being, King regarded federal government support as indispensable, his moral vision would, in the months not far ahead, bring him inexorably to a position of outright and unconcealed opposition to the Johnson administration. King's belief in nonviolence did not allow him to second the threatening urgency of James Forman; in response to another incidence (on the day after Johnson's address) of brutality on the part of Clark's possemen toward nonviolent demonstrators in Selma, Forman declared that SNCC was prepared to knock the "f—ing

legs" off the table of government if blacks were not allowed to sit at it. King would neither use such words, nor second their implication, but his outrage at the inequities of American society and the injustices perpetrated by its governing institutions was no less heartfelt than Forman's.

And for the present, there was evidence with which King could argue the efficiency of his tactics. In his address, Johnson had explicitly identified the civil rights movement's goals as one and the same as the most cherished American ideals of freedom and justice. Inspired by the selfless courage of the civil rights workers, the speech had constituted a milestone in the movement's history. "Never before, in nine

Shoved and dragged by policemen in Montgomery, Alabama, SNCC official James Forman stumbles toward a waiting patrol car. The fiery activist's arrest, one of many in his battle for civil rights, followed his organizing of black students to picket the state capitol.

On the march at last, protesters enter the last lap of their long trek from Selma to Montgomery. Among the thousands of marchers, all of them singing "We Shall Overcome" at the top of their lungs, are the Reverend Ralph Abernathy (third from left), Coretta Scott King, and her husband, Martin Luther King, Jr.

years time," according to David Garrow, "had the movement received the breadth of national support, and the strength of federal endorsement, that this week had witnessed. It was an emotional peak unmatched by anything that had come before, nor by anything that would come later." Johnson's speech "was a victory like none other," remembered C. T. Vivian. "It was an affirmation of the movement, it guaranteed us as much as anything could that we would vote and that millions of people in the South would have a chance to be involved in their own destiny."

Further affirmation came on Wednesday, March 17: citing an "almost continuous pattern of . . . harassment, intimidation, coercion, threatening conduct, and, sometimes, brutal mistreatment" on the part of Clark and his men, federal judge Frank Johnson gave the go-ahead to the Selma-to-Montgomery march. Led by King, 3,200 marchers left Selma via the Edmund Pettus Bridge on Sunday, March 21, protected there and en route by hundreds of federal marshals and national guardsmen. While Congress began hearings on the Voting Rights Act, the demonstrators tramped toward Montgomery along Highway 80. Through farmlands and cotton fields, pine thickets and ghostly swamps overhung with Spanish moss, they walked, said John Lewis, "with a sense of pride and a sense of dignity"; they were aware, remembered King's close friend and aide, the Reverend Ralph Abernathy, "that victory was in sight." After the first day, the group was reduced, by agreement with Judge Johnson, to 300 members, but on a rainy Thursday, March 25, as the procession entered the former Con-

Completing the four-day trek from Selma, civil rights demonstrators make a triumphant entrance in Montgomery on March 25, 1965. "We are on the move now to the land of freedom," said Martin Luther King, Jr. (holding the hand of his wife, Coretta, in the first row).

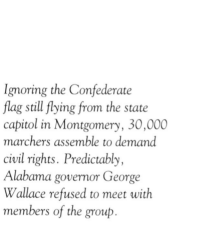

Ignoring the Confederate flag still flying from the state capitol in Montgomery, 30,000 marchers assemble to demand civil rights. Predictably, Alabama governor George Wallace refused to meet with members of the group.

federate capital city, its numbers multiplied many times over.

"We are on the move now," spoke King to the audience of 30,000 people arranged before a speaker's platform on the steps of the state capitol. "Yes, we are on the move and no wave of racism can stop us." There were many challenges still ahead—poverty, segregated housing, and the remnants of segregated education—and more "dark and difficult moments" waiting, he reminded his listeners, but victory was possible, and not far off. After all, he said in his mellifluous voice, the words coming out of him in long, rolling cadences, "there were those who said that we would get here only over their dead bodies, but all the world knows today that we are here." What we seek, he said, "is a society at peace with itself, a society that can live with its conscience." Interrupted many times by applause, he reached his climax: "How long will it take? I come to say to you this afternoon however difficult the moment, however frustrating the hour, it will not be long, because truth pressed to earth will rise again."

King's words now rose and fell in the call-and-response rhythm of the black church, so familiar to the experience of his listeners, itself a product of the music created by black field hands and slaves and convicts as they toiled. "How long?" King asked again. "Not long, because no lie can live forever." "How long?" he called; "not long," he responded, to the answering echoes of his aides, arrayed around him on the podium, "because you still reap what you sow." "How long? Not long. Because the arc of the moral universe is long, but it bends toward justice." "How long?" he asked again, and answered himself "not long" once more. He ended with the words of the "Battle Hymn of the Republic," the Union anthem during the Civil War, his use of the song clearly alluding to the long-standing nature of the grievances of the nation's black population and to the historical consequences of America's failure to fulfill its promise of freedom and justice for all. Suffused with hope, his listeners thundered out their belief. "It was like we *had* overcome," remembered Sheyann Webb. "We had reached the point we were fighting for, for a long time."

3

THE LONG, HOT SUMMERS

O N March 26—the day King spoke out in Montgomery—Viola Gregg Liuzzo, a sympathetic white housewife from Detroit, Michigan, was ferrying marchers from Montgomery back to Selma in her automobile. As she drove along Highway 80 that night, three members of the Ku Klux Klan shot her dead.

On August 3, 1965, just a little more than four months later, the U.S. House of Representatives passed the Voting Rights Act by a decisive vote of 326 to 74. The new law allowed the federal government to establish its own officials (in place of local registrars) and oversee elections and voting procedures wherever it could be demonstrated that discrimination in voting had occurred. The next day the Senate passed the bill by a similarly overwhelming majority, 79 to 18. Two days later, on August 6, President Lyndon Johnson signed the measure into law.

Hot, out of work, and out of patience, young black Newarkers taunt New Jersey national guardsmen during the summer of 1967. Like a number of other states in the late 1960s, New Jersey suffered recurring waves of violence in the ghettos of its major cities.

The passage of the legislation constituted the most significant victory of the civil rights movement. "Both the sponsors and the opponents of the Voting Rights Act agreed," says Robert Weisbrot in *Freedom Bound,* "that the new law bid fair to change race relations in the South more radically than at any other time since Reconstruction. Yet despite its far-reaching implications, the legislation enjoyed broader, more sustained public support than any previous civil rights measure. . . . Never before had the civil rights movement exercised so commanding or prestigious a position in national politics." Much of the credit belonged to King. In Selma he had been more successful than ever before in using the tactic of nonviolence to provoke the guardians of white supremacy into exposing its true character and moral failing—and a conscience-stricken nation could not fail to respond.

On August 11, 1965, five days after the Voting Rights Act became law, a 21-year-old black man named Marquette Frye was pulled over for drunk driving by a Los Angeles policeman in that city's black ghetto of Watts. In the 98-degree heat, the verbal confrontation between Frye and the officer grew increasingly hostile as a crowd formed on the street and police reinforcements arrived. Several of the white officers began swinging their nightsticks. Frye and his brother Ronald, who had come upon the scene, were clubbed to the ground and taken into police custody. When their mother, Rena Frye, protested their treatment, she, too, was arrested, as was another observer, 20-year-old Joyce Ann Gaines. In a hail of stones, bottles, pieces of pavement, and other debris, the police beat a retreat, while news of the incident,

inevitably embellished by rumor—one account had the police beating a pregnant woman—spread through the tense community.

For the next six days, 14,000 national guardsmen and several thousand policemen sought to restore order to Watts. Entire blocks burned while looters carried off merchandise from neighborhood stores. Snipers fired on policemen, and residents bombarded them with whatever they could hurl, including home-made Molotov cocktails. Thousands of blacks were arrested, 34 people were killed, thousands more in-

State troopers and Los Angeles police arrest a looter on August 13, 1965, the second day of trouble in the Los Angeles ghetto of Watts. The riots in the California city lasted six days, took 34 lives, injured thousands, and gave birth to the period's nihilistic motto: "Burn baby, burn."

With little seeming excitement, Chicagoans check out a new West Side blaze in 1968. The 1960s were studded with "long hot summers," steamy weeks of fury, looting, and out-of-control fires that raged intermittently through the poor black neighborhoods of the nation's big cities.

jured, hundreds left homeless, and scores of businesses destroyed. The total damage was estimated at $45 million, and "burn, baby, burn"—a slogan chanted by some of the rioters—became a kind of national watchword.

Most Americans found the violence of Watts shocking, but it was only the first—and by no means the worst—of a series of such outbreaks. In the previous summer similar but smaller-scale disturbances had broken out in northern urban ghettos in such cities as Rochester, New York; Paterson, Elizabeth, and Jersey City, New Jersey; Philadelphia, Pennsylvania; Chicago, Illinois; and New York City. In magnitude, however, the Watts riot set the style for four more long, hot summers.

In 1966, violence flared in the black communities of 38 American cities, most but not all of them in the Northeast. In 1967, large-scale disturbances occurred in 150 American cities, most significantly Newark, New Jersey, and Detroit, Michigan. In Newark during six days of rioting in mid-July, 26 people died and 1,200 were wounded in intense street fighting that pitted police and national guardsmen against ghetto residents.

The violence in Detroit, the nation's fifth-largest city, was even more intense—the worst, in fact, that had occurred in an American city in more than a century. Fires gutted more than 400 buildings. Forty-three people were killed, countless more injured. Soldiers went from building to building, rooting out snipers' nests and often, in their inexperience and fear, mistreating and brutalizing law-abiding residents. Federal troops and tanks prowled the burned-out west side, which looked, said Michigan governor George Romney, as if it had been bombed. Total damage was estimated at upward of $45 million.

Before this wave of urban violence began, Americans had been feeling self-congratulatory about the passage of civil rights legislation and various other ambitious social programs. Documenting President Johnson's ideal "Great Society," politicians, pollsters, and pundits churned out mountains of positive statistics about African Americans: 3 million blacks climbed above poverty level during the 1960s; twice as many blacks attained the then-middle-class annual income level of $15,000. Steadily fed such data, most Americans found the urban violence simply unfathomable, a wanton and inexcusable exercise in lawlessness out of all proportion to any possible provocation.

To the genuinely perceptive observer, the turmoil was more easily understood. Groundbreaking African American writer James Baldwin had dealt with the question in "Down at the Cross," an eloquent 1963 essay that examined the rise of the Nation of Islam. Here, Baldwin powerfully described his own lifelong struggle to overcome the "simple, naked, and unanswerable hatred" (sometimes defined by him as a "fever" or "rage in the blood"), which, he said, "no Negro living in America . . . has not felt" as a result of racism. Baldwin's prophetic essay warned America of "the fire next time" that would inevitably follow if the "relatively conscious blacks and the relatively conscious whites" failed to change American society. It was their mission, said Baldwin, to end America's "racial nightmare" and to create a society that recognized that "the value placed on the color of the skin is always and everywhere a delusion." These "conscious" Americans could succeed, Baldwin asserted, only through the implementation of "the most radical and far-reaching changes in the American political and social structure."

Baldwin, who was born in New York City's Harlem in 1924, was a friend of Forman, King, Malcolm X, Bayard Rustin, and many other civil rights leaders. A participant in several of the Selma demonstrations, he was by the mid-1960s perhaps the most famous writer in America. The "monarch of the literary jungle," as *Life* magazine titled him, commanded no small audience: after its initial appearance in the prestigious *New Yorker* magazine, "Down at the Cross" was pub-

Working in his Manhattan apartment in the mid-1960s, novelist, essayist, and social observer James Baldwin glances at a black madonna and child, an image characteristic of the era's emerging "black is beautiful" movement.

lished in Baldwin's essay collection *The Fire Next Time*, a book that remained a top national best-seller for a staggering 41 weeks in 1963. Baldwin thus reached perhaps more readers—many of them white—than any African American writer before him.

Still, a wide gap existed between blacks and whites in understanding black urban rage. It began with differing perceptions of how much progress had been made in reaching the goal that Baldwin had described in "Down at the Cross." Whites tended to point to civil rights legislation and the various Great Society programs as evidence of good intentions and positive action; blacks were much more acutely aware of what remained to be done.

In the two decades since the end of World War II—a period characterized by heavy black migration from the rural South to the urban North—the nation had enjoyed unparalleled economic prosperity. As a group, however, blacks still occupied the bottom rung of the economic ladder. Nearly half the nation's black families lived below the poverty level; the rate of black unemployment consistently stood twice as high as the white rate; and average black annual income amounted to slightly more than half of white income. Even education did little to narrow these disparities: in 1969, for example, the average income for a black American with eight years of schooling was $4,472; the figure for a white with the same amount of education was $7,018.

While the nation's prosperity was soaring between 1945 and 1965, the ratio of black family income to white family income climbed just 1 percent; between 1952 and 1963, that figure actually declined. By 1971, blacks still owned less than 1 percent of the nation's businesses. With such poverty came all the usual consequences: substandard housing in crowded, neglected urban areas; crime; substance abuse; health problems and heightened mortality rates; damaged family structures; limited educational opportunity for future generations; despair and the death of hope.

From the very beginning of life, the ghetto operated to shrivel expectations: in 1964, the infant mortality rate for blacks was 90 percent higher than it was for whites. With the increasing urbanization of the country's black population, the black rate had climbed 28 percent in the previous 14 years, a time when the rate should have been expected to drop dramatically because of vast medical advances. "Despite the court orders and laws, despite the legislative victories and speeches," said Lyndon Johnson in a 1964 address, for "the great majority of [black] Americans . . . the walls are rising and the gulf is widening."

To those in the North—who throughout the 1960s constituted approximately 40 percent of the nation's black population of 18 to 20 million—the specific achievements of the civil rights movement were less important than they were to southern blacks. Legal segregation was a southern institution, and northern blacks had long enjoyed access to the polls. Of greater concern to the northerners were longstanding practices of housing discrimination, which confined most urban blacks to bleak, hopeless ghettos, and a legacy of inadequate educational and economic opportunities, which imprisoned them in poverty.

> "The black cat in Harlem wasn't worried about no damn bus," said an official of the Urban League, a New York–based civil rights organization. (He was referring to the Montgomery bus boycott and the southern protests against segregation that followed in its wake.) "He'd been riding the bus for fifty years. What he didn't have was the fare." Using different words, a black New York City protester delivered a similar message in 1963: "I'd eat at your lunch counter—if only I had a job," read the words on his placard.

In deciding, after Selma, to devote his organization's efforts to the problems of poverty and segregated housing in the North, King had reached similar conclusions. With the fundamental constitutional rights of all black Americans now secured, in law if not yet always in practice, King believed it was time to focus on the other elements of true freedom and equality. What good is it, he asked rhetorically, to have the right to eat in a restaurant if one cannot afford the meal?

But King and other leaders would find that poverty was much harder to dramatize than southern segregation. Few persons of conscience could fail to see clear-cut injustice in the image of a black woman being clubbed by a white policeman because she wanted to vote, or in the sight of schoolchildren being blasted with high-pressure fire hoses for peacefully marching against segregation, or in the event of a group of peaceful demonstrators being mercilessly attacked by weapons-bearing law-enforcement agents.

Most Americans understood that blacks had the right to vote, and outside the South, a majority opposed legal segregation. Not all, however, were able or willing to admit that long-standing economic injustices had resulted in a form of de facto segregation in the North—in some ways even more damaging than overt segregation in the South. Fewer still realized that rectifying these economic injustices would require fundamental changes in the economy and massive government intervention in the form of social and economic programs.

In turning his attention to the issue of poverty and economic injustice, for example, King would propose a government-provided national minimum income for every citizen as a necessary first step. His trusted adviser Stanley Levison cautioned, however, that it would likely prove impossible to rally the same kind of broad-based black-white support around economic issues as had been mobilized for civil rights in the South.

The kind of coalition that had come together over Selma, advised Levison, was "basically a coalition for moderate change, for gradual improvements. . . . It is

militant only against shocking violence and gross injustice. It is not for deep radical change. The American people," Levison concluded, "were not inclined to change their society to free the Negro." And racism, as King already knew, was hardly confined to the South. In Chicago, where he led a largely unsuccessful campaign against segregated housing throughout much of 1966, he was moved to declare that he had "never seen anything so hostile and so hateful" as the white opposition he experienced there.

Whether due to a failure of conscience or understanding, this wide gap between black and white perceptions about black economic progress meant that for even most genuinely concerned whites, the explosion in Watts came as a shock. Casual observers saw

In Chicago to lead a housing-discrimination protest in 1966, Martin Luther King, Jr., staggers as a rock hits his head. Local whites attacked the black demonstrators with curses, stones, bottles, and firecrackers tossed at close range; King later said he had "never seen anything so hostile and so hateful."

in the Los Angeles neighborhood few of the usual indicators of urban decay. Its inhabitants lived in separate houses on tree-lined streets, not in towering, overcrowded apartment houses and housing projects. Watts residents enjoyed access to ample public facilities such as parks and swimming pools; the National Urban League even rated Los Angeles the nation's best city for blacks.

Those who lived in Watts, however, were more aware of the brutal day-to-day facts of life: a population density four times that of the rest of Los Angeles, an unemployment rate of 35 percent among adult males, two-thirds of the population on welfare, the frequent failure of such public services as garbage pickup, and the absence of public transportation connections with the rest of the city, which left the neighborhood an isolated enclave and severely limited employment opportunities.

Even more than Watts, Detroit had been seen as a model city for black progress and achievement. The availability of lucrative blue-collar jobs in its rapidly expanding automobile industry had made the city a magnet for the post–World War II black migration from the South, and blacks had established themselves in Detroit as in few other cities. Those who worked in the automobile industry were welcomed into the powerful United Automobile Workers Union, perhaps the most racially progressive such organization in the country.

At the time of the riots, Detroit was the only city in America represented by two black congressman. Its mayor at the time, Jerome Cavanagh, had been uncommonly successful in obtaining federal government funding for antipoverty programs. (Los Angeles, by contrast, was at the time of the Watts riots one of only two major cities without a significant antipoverty program in place.) Forty-five percent of Detroit's black families owned their own homes, a percentage unmatched elsewhere in the United States. Indeed, according to the sociologist Benjamin Muse, "There was probably more widespread affluence among Negroes in Detroit than in any other city in America."

But such prosperity existed side by side with the same kind of poverty and economic inequities that plagued other American cities. Few blacks in the automobile industry were allowed to rise to supervisory jobs in the plants or positions of influence in the union. Antipoverty programs, in Detroit as elsewhere in the nation, were insufficiently funded to relieve suffering significantly; Johnson's much-vaunted War on Poverty allocated, through the Office of Economic Opportunity (OEO), only from $50 to $70 per poor person. Welfare payments, the most frequently cited cause of white resentment of blacks, provided recipients with an income well below the amount the government itself defined as constituting poverty level.

The result in Detroit and the other urban areas of the North was described by Claude Brown in *Manchild in the Promised Land,* his searing 1965 autobiographical account of growing up in Harlem: "Too many people full of hate and bitterness crowded into a dirty, stinky, uncared-for closet-size section of a great city." Though black city-dwellers in the North might have been better off than they had been in the South, Brown wrote, the difference was one only of degree, and their situation was still dire: they "had gone from the fire into the frying pan." Those who had painted the North so brightly "had neglected to tell the folks down home about one of the most important aspects of the promised land: it was a slum ghetto. . . . The children of these disillusioned color pioneers inherited the

total lot of their parents—the disappointments, the anger. To add to their misery, they had little hope of deliverance. For where does one run to when he's already in the promised land?"

Brown's disappointment, disillusion, and anger, born of centuries of oppression, was no different than Baldwin's "fever" and "rage in the blood." According to Ron Scott, who was a 20-year-old auto worker in Detroit at the time of the riots there, "A lot of people felt it couldn't happen in Detroit, because people had good jobs, they had homes, and generally it was a good time, it was carefree, and people didn't have anything to worry about. But you can't always judge things by how they appear on the surface. Inside of most people there was a time bomb. There was a pot that was about to overflow, and there was rage that was about to come out."

If such emotions made the black neighborhoods of the northern cities a powder keg, nothing was more likely to ignite a conflagration there than the behavior of the police. Indeed, the majority of the urban upheavals during the long, hot summers began with some sort of confrontation between a white police officer and a black citizen. If, as Kenneth Clark and more radical analysts argued, America's black ghettos had become colonies of oppression amidst a land of plenty, it was no far stretch for their residents to view the police as an occupying army. In Watts and on the west side of Detroit, as in most black neighborhoods throughout the country, the police force was disproportionately white (200 out of 205 officers in the case of Watts) and, in the minds of most residents, racist if not notoriously brutal.

Under such circumstances, the most minor encounters could provoke an explosion: the rioting in Detroit began when police raided an after-hours drinking establishment in a black neighborhood. Baf-

fled by the size of the response to such seemingly trivial incidents, the police were unable to recognize that such encounters were merely the catalyst for a reaction to a much more far-ranging pattern of police conduct. "The riots will continue," said a young black man in Watts after the violence there, "because I, as a Negro, am immediately considered to be a criminal by police and, if I have a pretty woman with me, she is a tramp even if she is my wife or mother."

On one steamy Chicago day in the summer of 1966, the decision of an officer to shut off a fire hydrant where children were cooling themselves provoked violence that required 4,000 police to quell. The real cause of the rioting, however, was more likely to have been the community's unhappiness with, among other things, the department's policy of random stops and searches of black citizens—250,000 fruitless searches in the previous year alone. A year

A once-thriving Chicago business district smolders after two summer days of looting and arson by angry blacks. Most of the violence resulted from black rage about white police officers, who routinely stopped and searched African Americans simply because of their skin color.

earlier, James Farmer of CORE had characterized New York City's police force as a "paramilitary organization of 28,000 heavily armed men who killed 95 people last year"; many of those killed had been black.

In his essay "Fifth Avenue, Uptown," James Baldwin explained that "the only way to police a ghetto is to be oppressive." He continued:

> None of the police commissioner's men, even with the best will in the world, have any way of understanding the lives led by the people they swagger about in twos and threes controlling. Their very presence is an insult, and it would be, even if they spent their entire day feeding gumdrops to children. They represent the force of the white world, and that world's real intentions are, simply . . . to keep the black man corralled up here, in his place. The badge, the gun in the holster, and the swinging club make vivid what will happen should his rebellion become overt. Rare, indeed, is the Harlem citizen, from the most circumspect church member to the most shiftless adolescent, who does not have a long tale to tell of police incompetence, injustice, or brutality. . . . [The policeman] moves through Harlem, therefore, like an occupying soldier in a bitterly hostile country; which is precisely what, and where, he is, and is the reason he walks in twos and threes.

While many saw nothing more than random (and essentially self-destructive) violence in the northern riots, others discerned political content in the unchanneled expression of rage by urban blacks. To Baldwin, the riots were "slave revolts." To the black historians Lerone Bennett and John Hope Franklin, they were "urban insurrections." Underneath the "confusion and disorder," wrote Bennett, "was a wild kind of order that made Watts a major insurrection comparable in its day and time to Nat Turner's historic [slave revolt] 134 years before."

To Weisbrot, who is white, Watts was comparable

to the Greensboro sit-ins of 1960 that reinvigorated the civil rights movement and led to the creation of SNCC. "Watts," he wrote, "had triggered the resentments of ghetto residents as powerfully as four college students had stirred the hopes of southern blacks in 1960." To those who saw such actions as the looting of liquor and appliance stores as evidence of criminality rather than manifestations of political protest, the white sociologist Paul Jacobs responded, "Looting in the cities can be just as much an act of politics as it is a desire for goods. It is a way in which the poor can make a representation to the society, for they have no other kind of representation; it is a way in which the black poor can express their hate of the white world for not giving them their chance to share in the goodies."

Surprisingly, perhaps, the various committees empaneled by politicians to study the causes of the violence reached similar conclusions. Appointed by California's governor in the immediate aftermath of Watts, the eight-member McCone Commission was headed by the former director of the Central Intelligence Agency (CIA). This conservative group recommended a "revolutionary attitude" toward the problems of urban blacks in the form of education and job-training programs. "The existing breach [between whites and blacks], if allowed to persist, could in time split our society irretrievably," the commission prophetically stated. "So serious and so explosive is the situation that, unless it is checked, the August riots may seem by comparison to be only a curtain-raiser for what could blow up one day in the future."

Following the Newark riots, the Select Commission on Civil Disorders in New Jersey was appointed by the governor of the state. The "burden of responsibility" for the violence, declared the commission, "weighs most heavily on those in positions of leadership power and with control over the resources that will be needed to produce tangible results." There was nothing new about either the violence or its cause, the commission wrote; it was the same "unresolved issue" that had brought about the Civil War, the Chicago riot of 1919, and the Harlem riots of 1935: "the place of the Negro in American society." Indeed, one reason for the magnitude of the violence, concluded the commission, was that the legitimate grievances of blacks had gone unaddressed for so long. In the wake of the upheavals, the choice that faced the nation was "whether we shall resort to illusion, or . . . come to grips with reality."

Appointed by President Johnson and chaired by Illinois governor Otto Kerner, the 11-member National Advisory Committee on Civil Disorders was even more explicit. (Two African Americans— Edward Brooke of Massachusetts, the nation's lone black senator, and Roy Wilkins, the head of the NAACP—served on the commission.) "White racism" was the primary cause for conditions in the ghetto, the commission declared in its February 1968 report. "What white Americans have never fully understood—but what the Negro can never forget—is that white society is deeply implicated in the ghetto. White institutions created it, white institutions maintain it, and white society condones it." The United States was "moving toward two societies, one black, one white—separate and unequal." Unless checked, that movement would result in the "continuing polarization of the American community and, ultimately, the destruction of basic democratic values."

Though Johnson publicly distanced himself from the Kerner Commission's conclusions, privately he was more willing to concede their validity. "He's still nowhere," he said about the black man. "He knows it. And that's why he's out in the streets. Hell, I'd be there, too."

But whether proclaimed by civil rights activists,

expressed by demonstrators and rioters, or uttered by the leaders of their own political establishment, this message was not one that the majority of Americans were willing to accept. By 1963 polls consistently showed a large majority of Americans in favor of such goals of the civil rights movement as integration of schools and neighborhoods. But by the middle and later years of the decade pollsters recorded a majority of whites, even in the North, believing that blacks were "moving too fast" or "wanted too much."

Meanwhile, more and more Americans, the bulk of them young people, were joining in vociferous public protest against the country's escalating involvement in the Vietnam War. Older generations of whites watched the activities of their sons and daughters and grandchildren with profound unease. That moral repugnance, coupled with dread and disgust over the violence in the cities, soon led to widespread cries for "law and order."

Richard Nixon recognized a winning strategy when he saw one; what he saw in 1968 was a huge bloc of conservative white voters who feared and resented black progress and who regarded antiwar protests as unpatriotic. Nixon based his successful presidential campaign on appealing to this bloc, which he termed the "silent majority." His approach, wrote Republican political strategist Kevin Phillips, was based not on trying to unify American society but on "knowing who hates who." That same year, the once and future governor of Alabama, George Wallace—who had risen to national political prominence in the early 1960s by vowing "segregation now, segregation tomorrow, segregation forever"—utilized a strategy similar to Nixon's and made one of the strongest third-party showings in the history of American presidential elections.

This so-called white backlash was both a consequence and a cause of the widening split in the civil

rights movement. Divisive issues included the philosophy and practice of nonviolence, the growing
militance of the younger activists, and the tumult in
the inner cities. After Selma, King and the SCLC had
temporarily focused their attention on the North, but
SNCC kept its eyes on the South. Largely at the
instigation of the 24-year-old, West Indian–born
Stokely Carmichael, SNCC concentrated its efforts
in Lowndes County, Alabama, just east of Selma,
where, although blacks constituted four-fifths of the
county's population of 15,000, not one was registered
to vote. The state Democratic party's attitude toward
black voters—defined by its official motto, "White
Supremacy"—led Carmichael to encourage the
county's blacks to form their own political party, the
Lowndes County Freedom Organization. For its symbol, the new party took the black panther.

The imagery was significant. As John Hulett, who
became the first black in the county to register to vote
and who was elected sheriff of Lowndes County in
1970, explained, "The black panther was a vicious
animal who, if he was attacked, would not back up. It
said that we would fight back if we had to. . . . It was
a political symbol that we was here to stay and we were
going to do whatever needed to be done to survive."
During SNCC's time in Lowndes County the usual
pattern of white harassment, obstruction, and violence had prevailed: one freedom worker was murdered, and another seriously wounded (the assassin
was a deputy sheriff who was subsequently acquitted
by an all-white jury). As a result, and in contravention
of King's and Lewis's philosophy of strict nonviolence,
many of the new party's organizers armed themselves.

"Those of us who carried guns carried them for our
own protection, in case we were attacked by other
peoples," Hulett explained in *Voices of Freedom*.
"White peoples carried guns in this county, and the
law didn't do anything to them about it, so we started

carrying our guns, too. I think they felt that we was ready for war, but we wasn't violent. We wasn't violent people. But we were just some people who was going to protect ourselves in case we were attacked by individuals."

SCLC and SNCC (along with CORE) joined forces once more in June 1966 for a "March Against Fear" from Memphis, Tennessee, to Jackson, Mississippi, but the alliance was an uneasy one. The march had begun as an individual act of protest by James Meredith, who in 1962 (backed by thousands of federal troops) had become the first black student at the University of Mississippi. The purpose of his march was to encourage blacks in Mississippi to register to vote. On the second day of his trek he was felled by a white man with a shotgun.

Though badly wounded, Meredith survived his injuries, and the five major civil rights organizations

The leaders of the "Big Three" civil rights groups—left to right, Martin Luther King, Jr., of SCLC; Floyd McKissick of the Congress of Racial Equality (CORE); and Stokely Carmichael of SNCC— demonstrate their solidarity in 1966. In reality, the three disagreed sharply about policy: King continued to insist on nonviolence, while McKissick and Carmichael increasingly favored the use of "black power."

(SCLC, SNCC, CORE, NAACP, and the Urban League) vowed to continue his march. The last two pulled out, however, when Carmichael, who had replaced Lewis as chairman of SNCC, made a list of demands. He insisted that the Deacons for Defense, an armed self-defense group, be included; that there be no whites in a position of leadership for the demonstration; and that the march define itself as a "massive public indictment . . . of the government of the United States."

King still wanted to work with SNCC, but as the march progressed, tensions between the two groups worsened. The main cause was a new SNCC slogan, which Carmichael introduced at a rally on June 16 in Greenwood, Mississippi. The slogan—"Black Power"—drew an immediate, strong response from the public and the media. Never strictly defined, "black power" was, in the words of historian Allen Matusow, initially "less a systematic doctrine than a cry of rage." It expressed the impatience of Carmichael and other like-minded activists with having to rely on the benevolence of well-intentioned whites to attain those rights that should have been theirs as citizens of the United States.

The slogan also announced the activists' intention to rely on their own resources and abilities to obtain their rights—perhaps, in Malcolm's words, by any means necessary. "I'm not," said Carmichael, "going to beg the white man for anything I deserve. I'm going to take it." It declared the intention of such activists to rely strictly on black leadership, a declaration that would very soon put an end to the integrated structure of SNCC and CORE and lead to a purging

of its white members. It expressed the need for blacks to develop political and economic power, and to control schools, businesses, and other institutions in the black community itself. In the minds of some, it supported the notion of rejecting integration or even of developing a separate black nation, while for others, less drastically, it spoke to the notion of developing black pride in one's history, culture, and identity.

King was not opposed to many of the connotations of black power, particularly in its emphasis on pride and equality. But he had, in his own words, "immediate reservations" about the slogan. It was certain, he said—correctly—to frighten and alienate whites (notwithstanding the accuracy of the observation made by Carmichael, Baldwin, and numerous other analysts that blacks always had and still did have much more to fear from white power than whites did from black power).

King's unshakable commitment to nonviolence

Shoved off a public Mississippi highway during a 1966 voter-registration march, Martin Luther King, Jr., and his colleagues offer their usual passive resistance. The activists' plan—which they eventually carried out—was to complete the march begun by James Meredith, the pioneering integrationist who had been gunned down on the same highway earlier in the year.

made it impossible for him to endorse any program that seemed to sanction violence, besides which he found black power simply impractical as a strategy. As "we are ten percent of the population of this nation," he said, it was absurd to think "[we could] get our freedom by ourselves. There's going to have to be a coalition of conscience, and we aren't going to be free here in Mississippi and anywhere in the United States until there is a committed empathy on the part of the white man." Why, he asked Carmichael, choose a slogan "that would confuse our allies, isolate the Negro community, and give many prejudiced whites, who might otherwise be ashamed of their anti-Negro feeling, a ready excuse for self-justification?"

Other leaders were even more condemnatory. For Roy Wilkins, head of the NAACP, "black power" represented a "reverse Mississippi . . . the father of

Mississippi plantation workers watch participants of the 1966 March Against Fear, a voter-registration drive that led from Memphis, Tennessee, to Jackson, Mississippi.

Stokely Carmichael, elected head of SNCC in 1966, delivers a characteristically explosive speech in Seattle. The first to employ the slogan "black power," Carmichael had little use for King's philosophy of nonviolence: "I'm not going to beg the white man for anything I deserve," he thundered. "I'm going to take it."

hatred and the mother of violence." Coupled with often inflammatory rhetoric on the part of Carmichael and colleagues such as H. Rap Brown, the concept of black power, its opponents asserted, increased already existing white hatred of blacks and provided seeming justification for white backlash. The legitimate aspirations for freedom it expressed were immediately overshadowed by white fear of black violence.

In this context, the spontaneous urban insurrections of the long, hot summers were seen by many whites as the first manifestation of the call to black power. As its more militant offshoots gained in prominence, much of the once-strong white support for a nonviolent civil rights movement ebbed away.

4

RESPECT

IN early 1967, the various elements of the black freedom movement were debating the relative merits of integration, separatism, black power, and other issues. At the same time, musical history was being made at a recording facility in a small town in southern Alabama. On January 27, 1967, at the Fame Studio in Muscle Shoals, white producer Jerry Wexler of Atlantic Records was hoping to record 11 songs with the label's newest artist, a 24-year-old black female vocalist from Detroit, Michigan, named Aretha Franklin.

For a number of reasons, Wexler did not regard the session's success as a sure thing. Franklin had already recorded for five years with Columbia, the label to which she had been signed at the age of 18. Introducing her to Columbia had been John Hammond, the legendary talent scout who transformed American music through his discoveries; his finds included such important artists as jazz singer Billie Holiday; composer, bandleader, and pianist Count Basie; song-

"Queen of Soul" Aretha Franklin makes a record in the late 1960s. Born in 1942, the young singer skyrocketed to fame with the 1967 release of "Respect," a powerful song that seemed to speak for black America.

writer and vocalist Bob Dylan; and rock star Bruce
Springsteen.

Franklin's talent was an open secret in the music
industry, but although Hammond called her the
"greatest voice since Billie Holiday," her career at
Columbia had never really taken off.

When her contract with Columbia expired in
1966, Wexler quickly wooed her for Atlantic, a label
that had earned a solid reputation for success with
black artists, based most famously on the groundbreaking recordings it made in the 1950s with Ray
Charles, the blind pianist, vocalist, composer, and
arranger known at the label simply as "the genius."

**Charles filtered through his immense talent
elements of virtually every facet of American
popular music. He specialized in the blues,
gospel, spirituals, jazz, and rhythm and blues
forms of black America, but he also performed
country-and-western and even pop songs from
the Broadway stage and Tin Pan Alley. In all,
Charles created a unique hybrid that was dubbed,
for lack of another term, soul music. It was not
a term Charles much cared for, but most people
understood that it referred to the undefinable
emotional essence of the music—with its equal
parts joy and sorrow, humor and despair, longing
and regret, desire and parting, celebration and
loneliness, and ever-present emotional expres-
siveness and honesty. Charles himself called
the defining essence of his music "pure heart
singing."**

Wexler, who had produced Charles's best Atlantic
sides, hoped to replicate his success with Franklin's

recordings. She was, he observed, deeply rooted in the same musical traditions as Charles, and she was "searching for herself, not for external gimmicks." Born in Memphis, Tennessee, on March 25, 1942, Franklin had come north with her family in 1948. In Detroit, her father, the Reverend C. L. Franklin, became the pastor of the New Bethel Baptist Church and, in a short time, perhaps the most celebrated black clergyman in the country. A fine singer and a powerful, inspirational speaker, C. L. Franklin was famous nationwide for his sermons and services; eventually, he recorded more than 60 albums of his services and sermons.

The premier gospel singers of the day regularly performed at New Bethel and stayed in the spacious Franklin home. The family circle included the Five Blind Boys, Clara Ward, Sam Cooke and the Soul Stirrers, James Cleveland, the Staple Singers, the

Comprising the Mighty Clouds of Joy are gospel singers (left to right) Paul, Joe, Johnny, Richard, and Elmeo. Because the Clouds and other topnotch performers considered the Reverend C. L. Franklin's parsonage a second home, Franklin's daughter Aretha grew up surrounded by America's finest musicians.

Mighty Clouds of Joy, and Mahalia Jackson ("arguably the greatest vocalist of American popular music," according to music critic Dave Marsh). Franklin houseguests also included some of the greatest secular musicians of the time: jazz pianist Art Tatum, popular vocalist Dinah Washington, rock and roll pioneer Fats Domino, and blues singer Bobby Bland.

By the 1950s, Franklin's fame as "the man with the million-dollar voice" was such that he made frequent national tours, backed by the country's top gospel singers and groups. None of them, however, outshone the teenage Aretha Franklin, who had been singing at her father's services since her young girlhood. She began touring with him when she was just 14, the age at which she made her first recording: an inspired rendition of the gospel hymn "Precious Lord, Take My Hand."

In 1960, Aretha Franklin moved to New York City, where she spent five frustrating years recording for Columbia. During that time she became, through her father, a close friend of the Reverend Martin Luther King, Jr., to whom, according to Wexler, "she devoted an enormous piece of her life." An early supporter of civil rights and black pride, Reverend Franklin was one of King's most important northern supporters; in the summer of 1963, after the Birmingham demonstrations, he organized a massive Detroit SCLC support rally, which King had characterized as "the largest and greatest demonstration for freedom ever held in the United States."

At a similar rally for King and his group in Chicago that same summer, Franklin's daughter upstaged Mahalia Jackson and Dinah Washington with another stunning performance of "Precious Lord." "By the time [Aretha Franklin] finished" that night, wrote Taylor Branch in *Parting the Waters*, his history of the civil rights movement, "few [in the audience] doubted that for one night they had held the most favored spot on earth."

The first hit single from the Muscle Shoals session was "I Never Loved a Man," but the one that caused the greatest impact was "Respect." An assertion of female pride and self-sufficiency, the song also celebrates the beauty and independence of black women. In its most general sense, however, "Respect" was heard as an articulation of what blacks were demanding from American society, and it became a kind of anthem of the civil rights movement. For a while in the summer of 1967, the unforgettable, energizing opening chords of "Respect" seemed to be blasting from every open apartment window, car radio, and jukebox in America.

According to writer Thulani Davis, listening to Franklin sing in those days was as important to African Americans as hearing King preach. Her 1968 appearance on the cover of *Time* magazine represented a triumph of black American culture, specifically the musical forms that have been its most important expression. The *Time* cover, wrote Davis, "announced the mainstreaming of America's second truly indigenous musical form, rhythm and blues, and the complete crossover of the blues aesthetic into American popular culture." For poet Nikki Giovanni, Franklin was "undoubtedly the one person who put everyone on/notice . . . /Aretha . . . pushed every black singer into Blackness."

Franklin's accomplishments were part of a long tradition of African American artistic achievement. Music, an integral part of most African societies, has been equally central to African American culture. Created in fields, churches, homes, work camps, prison farms, juke joints, dance halls, and eventually concert auditoriums, African American music is one of America's greatest cultural achievements, and its practitioners are some of the nation's greatest artists. (James Baldwin often maintained that the true history of American blacks is written in black music.)

Indeed, virtually every kind of distinctly American music is rooted in black musical genres. What most observers regard as America's most important musical contribution, jazz, is an African American creation, derived from an older form, the blues (the music of rural southern blacks). The blues can, in turn, be traced backward to earlier older styles and practices, going all the way back to African song and dance, and forward, in rhythmically accelerated form, as the most critical element in America's perhaps most well-known musical creation, rock and roll. Likewise, the masters of pre–rock and roll American popular song, such white songwriters as the Gershwins, Rogers and Hart, Johnny Mercer, and Irving Berlin, often received their most inspired interpretations from Duke Ellington, Ella Fitzgerald, Billie Holiday, and other black jazz musicians.

Many of the giants of African American music were at work in the years between the Selma-to-Montgomery march and the formation of PUSH (People United to Save Humanity) in 1971. Edward "Duke" Ellington, for example, was still writing music and touring with his orchestra in the 1960s. Following the same road was William "Count" Basie, pianist, bandleader, and Ellington's longtime friendly rival in the competition to head the "best band in the land." With jazz—which whites once dismissed as "jungle music"—at last winning American recognition as a "serious" art form, both Ellington and Basie took their bands abroad in the 1960s, acting, at the request of the U.S. State Department, as American "cultural ambassadors." Their fellow jazz pioneer, trumpeter and vocalist Louis Armstrong, who was in large part responsible for the importance of the soloist and improvisation in the jazz tradition, also spent many seasons overseas.

During the 1950s, the pianist Thelonious Monk, Ellington's near-equal as a composer, had been revered as an esoteric, "underground" genius by a passionate but tiny band of jazz fans. By the 1960s, Monk was reaching a much broader audience as a Columbia recording artist. Armstrong's artistic descendant on the trumpet, John Birks "Dizzy" Gillespie, who with Monk and saxophonist Charlie "Bird" Parker had created the harmonically complex post–World War II jazz form known as "bebop," was still playing out often and recording prolifically. Bassist Charles Mingus, who proclaimed Ellington, Holiday, and Parker as his musical idols, was writing and recording some of the most enduring work of his career.

At the same time, players from an even newer generation—the most important among them groups

The face of Charles Mingus reflects the deep seriousness with which the celebrated jazz bassist approached his art. Mingus began his musical career in the 1940s, but he reached his full powers— both as a performer and as the composer of such works as Meditations on Integration—*in the 1960s.*

Brilliant guitarist Wes ("the Thumb") Montgomery took a new approach to his music in the 1960s; working with producer Creed Taylor, he began playing pop-radio and r & b songs as well as traditional jazz and bebop. His expanded repertoire greatly enlarged his audience and made him one of the era's outstanding performers.

led by the saxophonist Ornette Coleman and the pianist Cecil Taylor—were exploring the parameters of what they called "free jazz." This musical form, which emphasized almost total improvisatory freedom at the expense of such elements as melody and harmony, harked back to the music's roots in New Orleans. Its emphasis on complete artistic freedom and individuality was seen by many of its practitioners, listeners, and critics as reflecting and expressing the struggle of blacks to define themselves in American society on their own terms. Meanwhile, instrumentalist Wes Montgomery, who had demonstrated previously unimagined possibilities for the guitar, an instrument that had often been overshadowed in modern jazz—few of the most important and influential post–World War II groups used one—was laying

down the most successful commercial recordings
of his career.

> For many blacks, the ascendance of rock and
> roll as America's dominant popular music form
> served as a galling musical reminder of white
> cultural appropriation and economic exploita-
> tion. "I, too, hear America singing," wrote Julian
> Bond, a founding member of SNCC who in 1966
> was elected to the Georgia State Assembly
> (thereby demonstrating the importance of the
> Voting Rights Act). "But from where I stand,"
> continued Bond's poem, "I can only hear Little
> Richard and Fats Domino." In its conspicuous
> allusion to Walt Whitman, Bond's poem was
> intended as a reminder that blacks had as much
> of a claim to America's cultural heritage as did
> whites; more specifically, that if rock and roll had
> become, as often proclaimed, the "sound of
> America," the voices of blacks made up a large
> part of that sound.

Rock and roll had burst into the national consciousness in the mid-to-late 1950s when a trio of
white country boys recording out of Memphis—Carl
Perkins, Jerry Lee Lewis, and Elvis Presley—succeeded in crossing over from the country to the pop
charts with a handful of songs ("Blue Suede Shoes,"
"Whole Lotta Shakin' Goin' On," "Heartbreak Hotel," and others) that combined elements of country,
r&b, and the blues. All three recorded for the tiny Sun
label, whose owner, Sam Phillips, is often quoted as
having said that if he could find a white man who
could sing like a black, he could make a fortune.
Perkins and Presley were quick to acknowledge that
their music contained little that was genuinely new,

and that it drew heavily on black influences. Rock and roll, Perkins said, was little more than a "country man's song" played with the beat of black music.

In discussing his first single, "That's All Right Mama," which had been recorded earlier by black bluesman Arthur Crudup, Presley—soon to become one of the greatest phenomena in the history of American entertainment—allowed that his own efforts were but a pale imitation: "The colored folks been singing it and playing it just like I'm doin' now, man, for more years than I know. . . . They played it like that in the shanties and juke joints, and nobody paid it no mind till I goosed it up. I got it from them. Down in Tupelo, Mississippi, I used to hear old Arthur Crudup bang his box the way I do now, and I said if I ever got to the place I could feel what old Arthur felt, I'd be a music man like no one else."

White youngsters responded instantly to the new music. Rock and roll became the nation's newest musical craze and, in several years' time, its most dominant form of popular music. For blacks, there was bitter irony in the music's rise, for in many instances it seemed that the only thing new about this "new" music was that it was now being performed by whites for white audiences. Much of the new music did not sound much different from what black artists like Crudup and countless others even more obscure had been making for years, with few of the rewards that Presley and his musical children would reap.

If young whites immediately embraced rock and roll as a liberating force—"It was like busting out of jail," remembered white rocker Bob Dylan—its meaning for blacks was more complex. Black musicians such as Little Richard (the most outrageous and flamboyant live performer of them all), Fats Domino (a consummate pianist and musician rooted in the New Orleans tradition), and Chuck Berry (a superb wordsmith whose well-turned lyrics would establish

His showmanship almost obscuring his real musical talent, Little Richard delivers a trademark frantic performance. The artist helped create rock and roll, the blend of r&b, urban blues, gospel, and jazz that became the voice of the turbulent 1960s.

the guitar, the girl, and the car as perhaps the three dominant images in early rock and roll, and whose trademark guitar riffs would become one of the most recognizable signatures in rock and roll) were as inspired practitioners of early rock and roll as any of their white counterparts. In the late 1950s, however, the record charts were almost as rigidly segregated as the rest of American society. With music made by black performers confined to the "race" or r&b charts, black musicians had far less opportunity to cross over to the kind of commercial success enjoyed by Presley.

Indeed, many, such as Little Richard, watched as their r&b hits were covered by white artists for the much broader popular market. In many cases, the black originators of such music received no financial compensation for its appropriation. This trend continued in the early and mid-1960s, when the somewhat moribund American rock and roll scene was revived by the "British invasion"—the appearance in America of groups such as the Beatles, the Rolling Stones, the Who, the Animals, and Cream, all of them devotees of early rock and roll and especially the blues. The British rockers were uniformly generous in apportioning credit and recognition to their black inspirations—such as Berry, Little Richard, and blues-men Robert Johnson, Muddy Waters, Howlin' Wolf, Sonny Boy Williamson, John Lee Hooker, and Willie Dixon—which in some cases led to a resurgence in the black artist's career. Nevertheless, their success seemed to suggest a certain harsh conclusion to blacks: that to whites, their music was acceptable, even val-ued—especially to the extent that whites could profit from it—but that they personally were much less so.

It was in this context that the commercial success as well as the artistic achievement of Aretha Franklin, who both celebrated and was celebrated for her black-ness, became so important. Such recognition repre-sented not just financial reward for her talent and creativity but visibility for a people rendered too long "invisible," in the words of novelists Ralph Ellison and James Baldwin, in the eyes of the larger society. Frank-lin's progress was reflected in the accession of other blacks, in small but increasing numbers, to the boards of corporations, partnerships in law firms, surgical privileges in hospitals, management and ownership of businesses, and the classrooms of universities.

Because of the visibility it offered, success in the field of entertainment thus became especially important, and achievements that today might be regarded as commonplace or mundane were hailed at the time as milestones. Thus, the de-cision by Coca-Cola to use Franklin and Ray Charles for a national advertising campaign was

regarded as a significant development, for blacks had never before been used in such a prominent role as commercial pitchmen. Bill Cosby became the first black to win an Emmy Award (he actually won three in a row) for his dramatic work on the television series "I Spy," which debuted in 1965 and was the first network series to feature a black lead character.

In 1966, "Star Trek," a television series set, perhaps fittingly, far in the future in outer space, brought to America's TV viewers the first interracial kiss ever shown on the small screen (although many stations in the South refused to air the show on the night that Captain Kirk's and Lieutenant Uhura's lips met). Two years later, Billy Taylor, the accomplished jazz pianist and composer, became the first black to lead a band

Singing to his own piano accompaniment, Ray Charles cuts a record in the mid-1960s. Charles, often called simply "the genius" by those in the music industry, disliked the term "soul music," preferring to call his work "pure heart singing."

Miles Davis performs in New York City in 1972. The great jazz trumpeter accomplished what few others even hoped for: remaining true to his own musical roots, catering to no one, and still managing to become wealthy and famous.

on a television talk show when he agreed to direct the orchestra for the "David Frost Show."

The most important black musical artists of the period utilized a variety of strategies to deal with the reality of white control of the music industry. Some simply went their own way, making music that seemed totally unconcerned with, and uncompromised by, any commercial considerations. The supreme example of those who took this approach was jazz saxophonist John Coltrane. First prominent in the late 1950s as a member of Miles Davis's renowned group, Coltrane set out on his own in the early 1960s. By the time of his death from liver cancer at the age of 40 in 1967, Coltrane was regarded as perhaps the most "free" of the free jazz musicians and a kind of black patron saint of artistic integrity and individuality.

Coltrane's was a relentless musical quest to discover and express, in the words of his biographer Eric Nissenson, "ultimate language, the essence of music, the one great force, the mind of God, all braided and inseparable, swirling endlessly in the great cycle of the universe." Some critics, usually white, insisted on hearing in the frequent stridency and dissonances of Coltrane's later music the equivalent of the "anger" and "militance" of the most radical elements of the black freedom movement. Coltrane himself, however, always insisted that he was trying to express his personal understanding of the spiritual truths of the universe, which had to do with peace and unity. His musical legacy has rarely been equaled, and he remains one of the most influential and revered of all jazz musicians.

If Coltrane's individualism led him decidedly out of the jazz mainstream, his friend and onetime boss, Miles Davis, took a more complex approach to the prevailing currents in popular music. By the mid-1960s, the muted, lonely call of Davis's trumpet had long since made him the most famous, well-compensated figure in jazz, a position he had attained while making little concession to his audience. In live performance, he refused to introduce the material his group was playing, would not engage in onstage small talk, often left the stage while one of his colleagues soloed, and frequently played with his back to his audience—but he yearned for still more artistic independence.

Davis's onstage demeanor, for which he was often criticized, reflected his conviction that jazz should be treated as much as a serious art form as it was popular entertainment. He believed that a live performance

Jimi Hendrix makes a club appearance in the late 1960s. In his tragically brief life—he died of a pill overdose in 1970 at the age of 27—the flamboyant guitarist-singer-composer exerted a major influence on both the music and the lifestyles of the 1960s.

should be the equal of a recital in a concert hall; he was there not to entertain, but to be listened to. At the same time, in the late 1960s, after recording a number of brilliant albums, he became intrigued by the various possibilities offered by rock and roll. Disdainful of the limited musical abilities of most rock and rollers, Davis yet aspired to a similar level of mass appeal for himself and his music, and he believed that jazz should avail itself of the various technological possibilities the new music had pioneered, chiefly in the use of electronics and studio techniques such as overdubbing and tape editing.

Influenced by the guitar pyrotechnics of the newest sensation on the rock music scene, Jimi Hendrix, Davis also wished to restore the guitar—which he regarded as a quintessentially African American musical instrument—to a place of importance in jazz. And, as the years passed, he sought increasingly to emphasize what he regarded as the single most important element of all black music, rhythm. Although jazz purists howled when they heard the results—moody, atmospheric electronic masterpieces such as *In a Silent Way* and *Bitches' Brew*—other musicians followed in Davis's footsteps as they had throughout his long career, which dated to the late 1940s. By the early 1970s, electronic jazz-rock "fusion," the best of it played by Davis himself and disciples such as Wayne Shorter, Herbie Hancock, Tony Williams, Chick Corea, John McLaughlin, John Scofield, and Joe Zawinul, had become the "new thing" in jazz. Davis, meanwhile, was regularly playing in venues rarely frequented by jazz artists, often sharing the stage with rock and roll acts such as the Grateful Dead. He was now reaching, through both live performance and recordings, an audience larger than any ever commanded by a jazz musician, with little compromise to his artistry.

With predominantly white rock and roll swallowing up much black music and presenting it as its own, one black musician stood out as a reminder of rock's roots and a herald of its future. Born in 1942 in Seattle, Washington, left-handed guitarist Jimi Hendrix served his musical apprenticeship with a number of important black rock and roll, rhythm and blues, and blues acts—Little Richard, the Isley Brothers, B. B. King, James Brown, Wilson Pickett, Ike and Tina Turner, and King Curtis. By 1967 he had burst onto the rock and roll scene as head of a power trio, the Jimi Hendrix Experience.

In just three years—he died in 1970 as the result of an accidental overdose of sleeping pills—Hendrix completely revolutionized the use of the electric guitar. He melded elements of the blues and rhythm and blues with large doses of feedback and distortion, realizing a vision of his instrument's possibilities that jazz guitarist Larry Coryell described as "orchestral" in its simultaneous use of both rhythm and lead playing. Hendrix was a flamboyant showman; in concert he would play the guitar behind his back, behind his head, and with his teeth, and he sometimes set it aflame at the conclusion of a performance. Hendrix left a legacy of music as revolutionary in his own field as Coltrane's had been in his. Formally untrained, he was immediately recognized by contemporaries, especially Davis and other jazz musicians, as one of the most brilliant musicians of his day; guitarists are still attempting to duplicate his feats.

Perhaps Hendrix's most enduring artistic statement is the controversial, feedback-drenched rendition of the "Star-Spangled Banner" he performed at the conclusion of the famous Woodstock festival in August 1969. In the words of journalist Rob Partridge, the "number became a reference point for guitar players of the era keen to know just how much sound could be torn out of a guitar." Other listeners were attracted to the notes of social criticism and antiwar protest they heard as implicit in the sonic equivalent the guitarist produced for "the rocket's red glare" and "bombs bursting in air" of the national anthem's lyrics.

For Hendrix, who had done a two-year stint as a paratrooper with the 101st Airborne Division in the late 1950s, his version of the national anthem expressed both the pain and pride of being a black American: "I'm American, so I played it. They made me sing it in school, so it was a flashback, and that was about it. I thought it was beautiful." Many others disagreed, regarding his rendition as scandalous, disrespectful, and unpatriotic, the musical equivalent of the flag burnings and other "desecrations" engaged in by those protesting the U.S. involvement in the Vietnam War. No matter how one heard Hendrix, the question of what obligations black Americans owed their country, in terms of loyalty and patriotism, was to be at the forefront of the black freedom movement in the last years of the 1960s.

5

A DREAM DEFERRED

PROFOUNDLY divided as they were over the issue of black power and the role of whites within the movement, by 1967 SNCC and SCLC were agreed on one thing: the war in Vietnam was a disaster for African Americans. In some ways, their agreement on this issue bound them closer than their disagreements divided them. Their antiwar position drew the immediate condemnation of more conservative civil rights organizations, such as the NAACP and the Urban League, and antagonized and infuriated the Johnson administration.

SNCC officially condemned the United States's involvement in Vietnam in January 1966. The bulk of its membership, in keeping with its still nonviolent orientation, had been against the war from its outset, and some had spoken out individually. The most notable of these was Bob Moses, whose position anticipated the one that King and many other black analysts would take. He argued against the war not just from a general position of pacifism, but as a logical extension of his fight for equality as a black man.

Gathering at the Tomb of the Unknown Soldier in Arlington National Cemetery, a group called Clergy and Laymen Concerned About Vietnam holds a silent vigil in February 1968. Among the antiwar ministers, priests, and rabbis are the Reverend Martin Luther King, Jr. (center), and, at his left, the Reverend Ralph Abernathy.

SNCC chief Robert Moses, an early and vigorous critic of American involvement in Vietnam, explains some of his views in the early 1970s. U.S. hostility toward the dark-skinned Vietnamese, he maintained, was a mirror image of white southern hostility toward dark-skinned Americans.

Moses likened the mentality that allowed the United States to prosecute a violent war in Vietnam, whose people were mostly impoverished and of a darker skin color than white Americans, to that which allowed the violent repression of its own black population. In several antiwar speeches, Moses suggested that people needed to understand the reasons why the American public reacted so differently to the deaths of Jimmie Lee Jackson and James Reeb. Only then, he said, could one understand how America could be so indifferent to the suffering of the civilian population of Vietnam; the same forces were at work in the South and in Southeast Asia.

Even the visual images of the war suggested the connections between the two, Moses argued. To prove his point, he cited a newspaper photograph of a U.S. soldier with a captured enemy prisoner—"a little colored boy standing against a wire fence with a big huge white Marine with a gun in his back." The dark side of the national character that was revealed in the official lawlessness and violence that flourished in the South inevitably manifested itself overseas as well.

"The South has got to be a looking glass, not a lightning rod," said Moses. "You've got to learn from the South if you're going to do anything about this country in relation to Vietnam. . . . You can learn when it is that a society gets together and plans and executes and allows its members to murder and then go free. And if you learn something about that, then maybe you'll learn something about this country and how it plans and executes murders elsewhere in the world."

On January 3, 1966, Sammy Younge, a 21-year-old SNCC activist and navy veteran, was murdered for attempting to use a "whites-only" restroom in Tuskegee, Georgia. Three days later, SNCC issued its official statement about the Vietnam War, presenting arguments similar to the ones Moses had made. "The United States government has been deceptive in its claim of concern for the freedom of the Vietnamese people, just as the government has been deceptive in claiming concern for the freedom of colored people . . . in the United States itself," proclaimed the SNCC executive committee in its statement. (According to American antiwar activists, the United States had become involved in what was essentially a civil war in Vietnam. America claimed to be defending the "democratic rights" of the citizens of South Vietnam against "outside aggression" from the Communists of North Vietnam. The leader of North Vietnam, Ho Chi Minh, was, however, the democratically elected chief of the entire nation, North and South, a point the United States saw fit to ignore.)

"Younge was murdered because the United States

law is not being enforced," SNCC stated; "Vietnam-ese are murdered because the United States is pursuing an aggressive policy in violation of international law. The United States is no respecter of persons or law when such persons or laws run counter to its needs and desires."

King had indicated his disapproval of the Vietnam War on several previous occasions, but he did not make his major statement of opposition until April 4, 1967. Before that point, he had allowed himself to heed his advisers, who warned that speaking out would harm the cause of civil rights. Such a position, asserted the advisers, would permanently alienate not only the Johnson administration but a large segment of the population that might otherwise look with favor upon the black struggle.

By 1967 several factors had combined to prevent King from keeping silent any longer. First and fore-most was his belief in nonviolence, which compelled him to condemn the war as unjust by any standard. Moreover, in his analysis, the tactical considerations of his advisers no longer carried much weight. King was certainly aware of the potential consequences of public opposition, but in his mind the perils of silence were much greater: the war was already doing black Americans much more harm than could result from any statement he might make.

Though blacks constituted just 10 percent of the American population, they were 20 percent of the fighting forces in Vietnam and made up an even higher and more disproportionate percent-age of actual combat forces and casualties. Most were conscripts, not volunteers, despite the fact that, because of educational deficiencies, two-thirds of black 18-year-olds, as opposed to one-

Perched on an observation post in the South Vietnamese city of Hue, U.S. Marine sharpshooters watch for communist guerrillas in February 1968. Compared with their white counterparts, African Americans stood a much better chance both of being drafted and of getting wounded or killed in the war.

fifth of whites, failed the selective service exam. Predominantly white draft boards found ways around such difficulties, particularly in the South. There, observes Weisbrot, "young Negro male protesters were virtually guaranteed involuntary admission into the armed services." Young black males also stood a much higher chance of being drafted because, for various reasons, far fewer of them were enrolled in college, and college students at this time still received an exemption from the draft.

For King, the risk of alienating the Johnson administration was of much smaller consequence than it might have been several years earlier. The government was spending huge sums to prosecute the war in

Vietnam. It had become clear that if it continued to do so, it would not be able to fund the War on Poverty and other Great Society programs crucial to ending economic injustice—which, of course, King now regarded as the fundamental goal of his movement. "In a real sense the Great Society has been shot down on the battlefields of Vietnam," King told a reporter in early 1967.

In an address at New York City's Riverside Church on April 4, King was even more provocative. He had watched, he said, the poverty program "broken and eviscerated as if it were some idle plaything of a society gone mad on war." He had come to realize "that America would never invest the necessary funds or energies in rehabilitation of its poor so long as adventures like Vietnam continued to draw men and skills and money like some demoniacal destructive suction tube." How could he condemn the violence in the ghettos, about which Americans seemed to be so concerned, he asked, "without having first spoken clearly to the greatest purveyor of violence in the world today—my own government?"

The war, King asserted, amounted to taking the "black young men who had been crippled by our society and sending them 8,000 miles away to guarantee liberties in Southeast Asia which they had not found in Southwest Georgia and East Harlem. So we have been repeatedly faced with the cruel irony of watching Negro and white boys on TV screens as they kill and die together for a nation that has been unable to seat them together in the same schools."

King's war opposition represented a bold and even radical step. Previously, his actions on behalf of black civil rights always placed him in a position—no matter what the response of the white power structure that was threatened by his activity—with which few Americans could disagree. He was seeking, after all, nothing more than fundamental rights guaranteed all

Americans under the Constitution—ideals that each elected official of the federal government had sworn to uphold.

But now King had declared himself in a position of outright opposition to the government, and criticism and condemnation was immediate and widespread. With Johnson's approval, the FBI resumed its campaign against him, seeking to prove that his organization was led by Communists and that King himself was a "traitor to his country and his race." He was castigated in the nation's major newspapers and magazines, painted as being everything from simplistic to unpatriotic and disloyal. Roy Wilkins of the NAACP and Whitney Young of the Urban League condemned him, asserting their support for the president's Vietnam policy and their determination to keep the civil rights movement unsullied by antiwar protest. Black journalist Carl Rowan, who then held a position in the administration, publicly informed King that he could expect little support from the president in any of his work, for he was now "persona non grata to Lyndon Johnson."

SNCC, too, found itself isolated as the result of its antiwar position, but it had always been more willing to criticize the federal government, and its advocacy of black power had already moved it away from the mainstream. King's new outspokenness represented a more significant transformation, especially because of his immense prominence in American society. On April 30, King reiterated his antiwar message in a sermon at the Ebenezer Baptist Church in Atlanta. Among those in his congregation was John Lewis's successor as SNCC chief, Stokely Carmichael, who this time thrilled to King's words. He described the moment in *Voices of Freedom:*

> The speech was very beautiful. . . . He wants to, number one, first show that nonviolence has to be applied everywhere. It cannot just be segregated to the struggle of our

Uncle
Sam
wants
<u>YOU</u>
nigger

Become a member of
the world's highest paid
black mercenary army!

Support White Power
— travel to Viet Nam,
you might get a medal!

Fight for Freedom
. . . (in Viet Nam)

Receive valuable training
in the skills of killing off
other oppressed people!

(Die Nigger Die — you can't die
fast enough in the ghettos.)

So run to your nearest recruiting chamber!

Working an Atlanta, Georgia, street corner in 1967, a young Stokely Carmichael hands out satirical leaflets (right) to discourage blacks from enlisting in the U.S. military. The nation's civil rights workers were almost universally opposed to the Vietnam War.

people inside the United States. He wants to also show that it must be a vital force in the world politics and in world struggle. . . . So what he comes to do is to link together the struggle of the Vietnamese and our struggle in a clear sense. He comes to show the necessity to stand up against your own government, to take a proper stand against the government if the government is incorrect. . . . His breaking of man-made laws were breaking of southern laws . . . which everybody had to condemn. But going against the United States government is another issue. As a matter of fact, he depended upon the United States government in . . . his struggle against breaking the laws of the South. But when you go against the United States government, there's nobody upon whom he can call, except God, to help them seriously in his struggle.

So here, whether he knows it or not, he was taking the conscience of his people, not just against the southern sheriff, not against Bull Connor, but now against the entire policy of the United States government. . . . So his church understood precisely the struggle in Vietnam, the necessity of nonviolence to be applied there. The necessity of them to heighten their consciousness against the war in Vietnam, using their experiences from their own struggle against racism, and they came to understand properly that this position would put him in a most unpopular position and would lead him into complete confrontation with the forces. They understood completely.

Stung as he was by the criticism that poured down on him following his April 1967 antiwar statements, King was not totally surprised. He was growing increasingly disheartened by the direction American society was taking: the violence in the nation's ghettos; white society's apparent indifference to treating its underlying causes; the war in Vietnam; the lack of success of his efforts in Chicago; congressional cuts in

As a newsman records the 1964 scene, restaurateur Lester Maddox evicts two young black men who had tried to integrate his Atlanta cafeteria. Rather than disgusting his fellow Georgians, Maddox's much-publicized racism earned him the state governorship in 1966.

*Mayor Carl Stokes of
Cleveland, Ohio, holds
a postelection press conference
in November 1967. Stokes,
the first African American to
take the helm of a major U.S.
city, had declined the campaign
assistance of Martin Luther
King, Jr., fearing that King's
passionate opposition to
the Vietnam War would drive
away conservative voters.*

poverty programs and rejection of national open-housing legislation; and various manifestations of white backlash. The most appalling of these was the election as governor of Georgia of Lester Maddox, whose chief qualification for office was that he used an ax handle to chase away blacks who attempted to eat in his Atlanta fried-chicken restaurant. (Maddox also bought newspaper advertisements in which he encouraged whites to come to Atlanta to "hunt" blacks.)

All this moved King closer to despair as 1967 wore on. Not even the November 1967 election in Cleveland, Ohio, of Carl Stokes as the nation's first black mayor of a major city, significant achievement as this was, did much to lessen King's growing sense of discouragement: for fear of white backlash among the city's voters, Stokes found it necessary to ask King and other civil rights leaders to take a minimal role in the campaign.

King's statements, as on Vietnam, grew more explicit, more directly critical than at any other time in his life in the public eye. "The Negro is not moving too fast," he said; "he is barely moving." He had grown dubious about the good intentions of whites; most of them were "not committed to equal opportunities for Negroes," he said. "America has been, and she continues to be, a racist society."

Urban riots, said King, "are caused by nice, gentle, timid, white moderates who are more concerned about order than justice" and "by a national administration more concerned about winning the war in Vietnam than the war against poverty right here at home." He saved some of his harshest condemnations for Congress, where legislators such as House minority leader Gerald Ford (who would eventually succeed Richard Nixon as president) were engaged, as they trimmed social programs, in speculation as to whether the urban riots were in fact some kind of national communist conspiracy. "How long are we going to abdicate law and order—the backbone of civilization—in favor of a soft social theory that the man who heaves a brick through your window or tosses a fire bomb into your car is simply the misunderstood and underprivileged product of a broken home?" asked Ford.

"The tragic truth," said King, "is that Congress, more than the American people, is now running wild with racism." It was no longer time to "beg Congress for favors," said King, "but to create a situation in

Youngsters at a Black Panther–sponsored "liberation school" demonstrate the Black Power salute in 1969. Believing that African American youth needed to learn pride and self-reliance, the Panthers opened a network of schools to prepare the children for their roles as "soldiers and educators."

Members of the militant Black
Panther Party protest the
imprisonment of their founder,
Huey P. Newton, with a New
York City parade in July 1968.
Organized in California in 1966,
the Panthers advocated black
self-determination and armed
self-defense against the
oppressive white "establishment."

responsibility and decency." Believing that America was "engaged in two wars and losing both," he began contemplating ways to organize a program of nonviolent but massive civil disobedience in the North—boycotts, marches, sit-ins—that would "cripple the operations of an oppressive society." Blacks, he said, were rightly "not in a mood to wait for change by the slower, tedious, often frustrating role of political action."

As Young and Wilkins made clear, King did not speak for all blacks, especially on Vietnam. Either out of sincere conviction, economic necessity, or coercion (in the form of the draft) tens of thousands of African Americans served with great distinction in Vietnam, and some at home supported the war and the president's policy, on Vietnam and other matters. In the 1968 presidential election, several prominent blacks—basketball star Wilt Chamberlain, the phenomenally popular entertainer Sammy Davis, Jr., and baseball trailblazer Jackie Robinson—and a small number of less well known black voters supported the Republican candidate, Richard Nixon.

For others, King was still not radical enough. Carmichael and his successor at SNCC, H. Rap Brown, made pronouncements in favor of violence (which was, said Brown, "as American as apple pie"). Brown even urged the shooting of whites, and a new group formed in Oakland in 1966, the Black Panther Party (which took its name from the symbol for the new political organization formed by black voters in Lowndes County in 1965), advocated armed self-defense against white oppression and went so far as to carry rifles into a session of the California state legislature.

Even so, King's leadership had never seemed more dynamic, relevant, and important, and his increased outspokenness won for him a new level of support and respect, especially among young blacks in the North. "I'm not nonviolent myself," Weisbrot quotes a young urban black as saying about King at this time, but King "was definitely in touch with the people because he had changed his stand, he had become more militant and everyone could see this." According to Weisbrot, "such ghetto dwellers accepted King for the first time, as they saw him moving—much like Malcolm before him—toward higher, revolutionary ground."

6

KEEPING HOPE ALIVE

FOR all Martin Luther King, Jr.'s stature, he was not the most visible symbol of black opposition to the Vietnam War. Strangely enough, that distinction belonged to an athlete: heavyweight boxing champion Muhammad Ali. That an athlete should occupy a place of such importance is less surprising when one considers that sports—like music and other forms of entertainment—had for some time constituted one of the few avenues of achievement open to blacks within the larger society.

In the 1960s, as television and the impact of the big money it brought in its wake began a radical transformation of the professional sports world, its best performers attained an ever greater level of prominence and visibility. For King and many others, the achievements of black athletes were one and the same with the overall struggle of blacks for freedom and equality. "You'll never know what you and Jackie and Roy did to make it possible to do my job," he told retired pitcher Don Newcombe, who with his Brook-

World Heavyweight Champion Muhammad Ali talks to young admirers in the Roxbury section of Boston, Massachusetts, in April 1964. Just two months earlier, the boxer had astonished the nation by dropping his "slave name," Cassius Clay, and announcing his membership in the Nation of Islam.

121

lyn Dodgers teammates Jackie Robinson and Roy Campanella had helped integrate major league baseball in the late 1940s. Though such sports as major league baseball and professional basketball opened their doors to blacks relatively late (baseball in 1947, basketball in 1955), by the mid-1960s black American athletes dominated virtually every sport in which they competed, thereby achieving a significant degree of fame within the larger society.

> **In baseball, for example, the three best all-around players in the game—Willie Mays, Roberto Clemente, and Hank Aaron—were African Americans. Aaron was on his way to setting the all-time record for most home runs in a career, besting the mark set by the hallowed Babe Ruth (and in the process receiving a deluge of racist condemnation and threats). Another African American star, outfielder Frank Robinson, would in 1966 win the rare Triple Crown while leading his team, the Baltimore Orioles, to the world championship and becoming the only player in major league history to win the Most Valuable Player award in both leagues. The fiercely competitive and intelligent Robinson went on to hit more home runs in his career than all but three players (Aaron, Ruth, and Mays) and achieved an even greater milestone in 1975, when he became the first black manager in the history of major league baseball.**

In 1968, black pitcher Bob Gibson, enjoying the greatest season in a storied career that would lead to his being enshrined in the game's hall of fame, set the record for the lowest earned-run average (or ERA, the single best measure of a pitcher's effectiveness) for a

Henry Aaron became baseball's all-time home run king in 1974, when he socked the 715th homer of his career and broke Babe Ruth's record. The slugger's easygoing manner and astounding athletic abilities brought him adoration from both black and white fans, but his overtaking of a white hero's legend also triggered attacks of vicious racism.

season. Throughout the late 1960s, outfielder Lou Brock was blazing his way to an all-time mark for stolen bases in a career. In any measurement of the game's best performers, be it the rosters for the annual All-Star game or simply a list of league leaders in various categories, blacks were represented in numbers far higher than their percentage of the general population would have indicated, as indeed they were in sheer number of performers at the major league level.

Off the field, one the most significant developments in the game's history was also initiated by a black player, Curt Flood, the thoughtful, graceful center fielder of the St. Louis Cardinals. Flood sacrificed his career by bringing a lawsuit that challenged major league baseball's reserve clause, which bound players in perpetuity to the team that originally signed them at the sole discretion of that organization's management. Though Flood lost his suit, his heroic act inspired others to challenge the reserve clause, which was abolished in the early 1970s, giving sufficiently talented players the right, as so-called free agents, in effect to choose their own employer. The direct result was the kind of stratospheric salaries players are paid today.

Black dominance of professional basketball was even more pronounced. In the spring of 1969, Bill Russell concluded his remarkable career in the National Basketball Association (NBA) by leading his team, the Boston Celtics, to its unmatched 11th championship, all of them won in his 13 years with the team. Russell's valedictory achievement was all the more significant in that in his final season he served his team not only as its center, but as its head coach as well—the first black head coach in the NBA's history. By that point, well over half of the league's players were black; today's figure is close to 90 percent.

Included among that figure was a disproportionately large number of the game's best performers. Russell's great rival at the center position, Wilt Chamberlain, an unprecedented combination of size, strength, and grace, was in the prime of a career that would end, among myriad other achievements, with his grabbing more rebounds and scoring more points than any player in history. (At the time of the Selma-to-Montgomery march, the man who would break Chamberlain's career scoring record, Kareem Abdul-

Jabbar, then a skinny schoolboy named Lew Alcindor, was at work on the playgrounds and in the gymnasiums of New York City perfecting his trademark "sky-hook" shot.)

Forward Elgin Baylor, meanwhile, had by the mid-1960s forged a legacy of high-flying acrobatics and scoring feats that established him as the rightful basketball ancestor of Michael Jordan. In the backcourt, Oscar Robertson, the league's perennial leader in assists, was generally acknowledged as the game's best guard. Today's basketball fan, familiar with the criteria of the triple-double (double figures in three separate statistical categories) as the accepted standard of rarest excellence for a single game's performance, might well marvel to learn that Robertson averaged a triple-double (in scoring, assists, and rebounds) over the course of several seasons. Equally important, off the court Robertson was a pioneering president of the league's players association and was instrumental in bringing free agency to the NBA. (By the mid-1990s, the NBA Players Association had established itself as the most enlightened and effective of any of the major sports league's unions.)

There were many other black stars as well, as in baseball too numerous in all to mention; collectively they and their successors were responsible for transforming the game's style to one that emphasized quickness, athleticism, and individual style and ability within the team framework. In the process, they elevated professional basketball to the position of immense popularity that it enjoys today. Indeed, just as no sport in America has been so black-dominated, no sport holds as important a place within African American culture.

Given the times, it was perhaps inevitable that many among this generation of black athletic heroes would speak out on social and political issues. Russell, a tireless supporter of the civil rights movement, received much criticism for his characterization of Boston as the "most racist city in America" at a time when its white establishment was naively proud of its "progressiveness" on racial issues. Alcindor, by then an undergraduate at the University of California at Los Angeles, saw his popularity suffer when he declined to play for the U.S. team at the Summer Olympic Games in Mexico City in 1968. A few years later, his popularity declined even further when he announced his conversion to Islam and his decision to take an Islamic name, Kareem Abdul-Jabbar. (Members of the Nation of Islam take Islamic names to replace their given or "slave" names, which can presumably be traced back to names given their ancestors by white slaveholders.)

During the Vietnam years, polls revealed an ever-increasing number of blacks who stated that, given the prevailing racial situation, the United States was not worth fighting for. Alcindor was but one of several world-class black American athletes who found that they could not in clear conscience represent their country at the Olympic games, which tended to serve as a vehicle for unquestioning American patriotism as well as for athletic competition.

The patriotism element received a clear demonstration from two black athletes who did compete in the Olympics. The sprinters Tommie Smith and John Carlos used the public forum provided by the games to offer their own form of nonviolent protest. After finishing first and third, respectively, in the 200-meter run, Smith and Carlos removed their shoes, covered their right hands in black gloves, and, during the playing of the "Star-Spangled Banner" that accompanied the awarding of their medals, bowed their heads and raised clenched fists in a Black Power salute. The

*Tommie Smith (center) and John Carlos (right center)
make Olympics history with a black-gloved Black Power salute at the 1968 games, held in Mexico City. The gesture cost both U.S. champion sprinters their medals.*

outcry from the American public was immediate, and the United States Olympic Committee stripped the athletes of their medals. Boxer George Foreman, by contrast, made himself a hero by waving a tiny American flag in the ring after winning a gold medal in the heavyweight division at the same Olympics.

None of these athletes, however, aroused the same degree of enmity or inspired the same level of adulation as did Muhammad Ali. Prodigiously gifted in the ring, with a speed and grace never before seen in a fighter his size (Ali stood six feet, three and one-half inches tall, and in his prime weighed between 210 and 225 pounds), stunningly handsome, brash, witty, and charismatic, Ali was controversial—and reviled by many whites—long before he spoke out against the war. In an age when white Americans expected black athletes to be modest and soft-spoken, Ali made a habit of predicting, in poetry, the round in which he would knock out his opponent and of proudly expounding on his good looks—"I'm so pretty"—and his ability—"I am the greatest of all times."

In a lesser fighter, Ali's statements might have been dismissed as eccentricity or clowning. To the dismay, however, of the many white fans who regularly rooted for his opponents to silence the Louisville Lip (he was born Cassius Marcellus Clay in Louisville, Kentucky, in 1942), Ali had the ability to go with his boasting. He combined speed with power and truly could, as he often proclaimed, "float like a butterfly and sting like a bee."

After winning a gold medal in the 1960 Olympic Games (and, after enduring yet another racial insult in his segregated hometown, tossing it in the Ohio River), the still relatively inexperienced Ali—he had fought just 19 professional opponents—shocked the sporting world by defeating the fearsome and heavily favored heavyweight champion Sonny Liston in February 1964. The very next day, the new heavyweight champion of the world further stunned white America when he announced that he was a member of the Nation of Islam and would henceforth be known as Muhammad Ali.

Counseled by Malcolm X, who called him his "younger brother," Ali had in fact been a member of the Black Muslims since 1961. Sportswriters were virtually unanimous in denouncing him, and he was insulted regularly in the nation's newspapers, where he was persistently identified only by his "slave name" of Cassius Clay. Overnight, in the eyes of many, the mildly annoying but likeable Cassius Clay had become (in his own words) a "loudmouthed nigger" named Muhammad Ali.

But controversy could not silence Ali's braggadocio, which served a dual purpose. Number one, it was great box office. Heavyweight boxing had a long tradition of matching cocky black fighters—most notably Ali's idol, the early 20th-century champion Jack Johnson—with so-called "great white hopes"—boxers who fought to silence such black braggarts and restore white honor. (In the absence of a sufficiently talented white fighter, a compliant black could be used as a surrogate. In the mid-1960s, for example, Ali fought Floyd Patterson and Ernie Terrell. Both insulted him, and earned the allegiance of white fans, by refusing to address him as anything other than Cassius Clay. Outside the ring, Ali labeled both as "Uncle Toms"; in the ring he cruelly punished them, refusing to administer a merciful knockout blow to the badly injured fighters while taunting them—"What's my name?"—with every lightning punch that he landed.)

Ali, boxing's top draw virtually from the beginning of his career, recognized that one could make a profit by playing the villain in such racist scenarios: "I knew that to draw money to me—people, rich people, mainly the white people at the time, could buy ringside seats—I had to act crazy supreme. 'I am the greatest of all times. I'm pretty. Talk jive and walk in five.' They said, 'The nigger talks too much. Nigger needs a good whuppin.' " White fight fans scrambled for tickets.

More important, Ali's unshakable self-confidence served as a very public display of black pride, a most visible (and audible) equivalent of slogans such as "black is beautiful" and "I'm black and I'm proud, say it loud." Such phrases (along with "Afro" or "natural" hairstyles, African fashions, an emphasis on the African heritage of black Americans, and, indeed, the use of the term *black* in place of *Negro*) came into vogue with the beginnings of the black power movement.

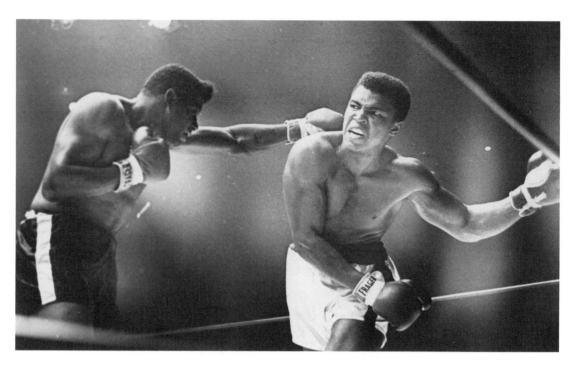

A snarling Muhammad Ali easily ducks a punch aimed by Floyd Patterson during a scheduled 15-round title bout in Las Vegas, Nevada, in 1965. One of those who mocked Ali's new name, Patterson paid for his taunts; after pounding him unmercifully, Ali decked the former champ in the 8th round.

"That's what made me so attractive," Ali said. "A black man said 'I'm the greatest.' We [blacks] weren't taught like that. We were taught the black man had the bad luck. Black was bad and white was good. So me, being black—'I am the greatest. I'm pretty'—it gave more people confidence and it put me in such a spot. I had to fight to back up my words."

Through March 1967, Ali had fought 29 fights and won them all. At that point he was at the peak of his superb athletic skills, "so breathtakingly dominant," in the words of biographer Thomas Hauser, "that even his detractors were forced to admit his skill. His bouts had become performances rather than contests. He was so good, it seemed he might never lose." Then came his toughest fight—with the U.S. Selective Service, which administered the draft of eligible young men for the armed services. More than a year earlier, Ali had been notified that he was being made eligible for the draft. His immediate reaction had succinctly and eloquently summarized what an increasing number of Americans, black and white, many of them young, had come to feel about the war.

> **Announcing his intention to refuse induction into the military, Ali said, "I ain't got no quarrel with them Vietcong," and earned a new round of vilification from the press and the public and surveillance by the FBI. "No Vietcong ever called me nigger," he would later further explain, and he sought, citing his Islamic beliefs, to be relieved from military service as a conscientious objector. "Why should they ask me to put on a uniform and go ten thousand miles from home and drop bombs and bullets on brown people in Vietnam when so-called Negro people in Louisville are treated like dogs? If I thought going to war would bring freedom and equality to 20 million of my people, they wouldn't have to draft me; I'd join tomorrow. But I either have to obey the laws of the land or the laws of Allah. I have nothing to lose by standing up and following my beliefs. So I'll go to jail. We've been in jail for four hundred years."**

On April 28, 1967, Ali was ordered to report for induction into the military at the U.S. Armed Forces Examining and Entrance Station in Houston, Texas. At the center, he refused to step forward when his name was called, whereupon he was notified that he was committing a felony punishable by up to five years in prison. His actions unleashed a new paroxysm of hatred for him in the media. The term "draft dodger" was added to the various epithets applied to him, and he was immediately stripped of his title and denied a license to practice his livelihood in all 50 states of the union.

Many, however, were inspired by the substance and character that Ali had shown beneath his flamboyant public persona. "That day in Houston," he later remembered, "I felt happy. . . . The world was watching, the blacks mainly, looking to see if I had the nerve to buck Uncle Sam, and I just couldn't wait for the man to call my name, so I wouldn't step forward." In June 1967, on the eve of his trial, several of the nation's most prominent black athletes met with him to demonstrate their support.

For Kareem Abdul-Jabbar, who was among those who attended the meeting, Ali was a "hero . . . whose impact on young people was formidable." For the much revered Bill Russell, Ali represented a kind of ideal for black people. "I never thought of myself as a great man," Russell later said. "I never aspired to be anything like that. I was just a guy trying to get through life. But in Cleveland, and many other times with Ali, I saw a man accepting special responsibilities, someone who conducted himself in a way that the people he came in contact with were better for the experience. Philosophically, Ali was a free man. Besides being probably the greatest boxer ever, he was free. And he was free at a time when historically it was very difficult to be free no matter who you were or what you were. Ali was one of the first truly free people in America." At the time, Russell told the press how he felt about Ali: "He faces a possible five years in jail and has been stripped of his heavyweight championship, but I still envy him. He has something I have never been able to attain and something very few people I know possess. He has an absolute and sincere faith. I'm not worried about Muhammad Ali. He is better equipped than anyone I know to face the trials in store for him. What I'm worried about is the rest of us."

On June 19, 1967, Ali was convicted and sen-
tenced to five years in jail, though he remained free
pending appeal. For the next three and a half years, as
his case made its way through the courts, he was
denied the right to fight. Instead, he earned his living
by giving lectures on college campuses, where he
became the nation's most visible antiwar spokesman.
In June 1971, the U.S. Supreme Court unanimously
overturned his conviction, ruling that the government had erred in denying him conscientious objector
status. Eight months earlier, he had returned to the
ring, in Atlanta, Georgia, against Jerry Quarry, a fight
that Julian Bond described "like nothing I've ever
seen. The black elite of America was there. It was a
coronation; the King regaining his throne. . . . It was
more than a fight, and it was an important moment
for Atlanta, because that night, Atlanta came into its
own as the black political capital of America."

Ali won that night, though five months later at
New York City's Madison Square Garden, in perhaps
the most ballyhooed sporting event in American history, he suffered the first defeat of his career to Joe
Frazier, the similarly undefeated heavyweight who
had taken his place as champion. Subsequently, he
would defeat Frazier twice and reclaim the championship (the first heavyweight ever to do so) in 1974 by
defeating George Foreman. In the remaining seven
years of his career he went on to lose and regain the
championship a third time while attaining a level of
fame that left him generally acknowledged as the most
universally recognized person on the planet.

For singer, actor, and civil rights activist Harry
Belafonte, Ali "was, in many ways, as inspiring as Dr.
King, as inspiring as Malcolm. . . . Muhammad Ali was
the genuine product of what the movement inspired.
He was the best example. He was the Negro kid who
came up in the time of the black movement. Who was
Cassius Clay in the beginning and became Muham-

mad Ali in the end. He took on all the characteristics and was the embodiment of the thrust of the movement. He was courageous. . . . He brought America to its most wonderful and its most naked moment. 'I will not play in your game of war. I will not kill in your behalf. What you ask is immoral, unjust, and I stand here to attest to that fact. Now do with me what you will,' he said. And he was terribly courageous, he was powerful, he was the embodiment of the new day and was very inspirational."

Ali was one of the fortunate few to receive a kind of justice, poetic and legal, in his own lifetime. Other prophets, however, must endure martyrdom. On April 4, 1968, Martin Luther King, Jr., was shot and killed by a gunman (escaped white convict James Earl Ray) as he stood on the balcony of a motel in Memphis, Tennessee. King had come to support a strike by the city's black sanitation workers, and just the night before he had given one of his most powerful speeches. He had assured his listeners of the ultimate justice of their cause while seemingly foretelling his own death: "I may not get there with you, but I want you to know tonight that we as a people will get to the promised land."

A host of the nation's most important political leaders, dignitaries, and celebrities packed Atlanta's Ebenezer Baptist Church for King's funeral services, where Aretha Franklin sang "Precious Lord." Afterward, thousands of the common people whose lives he had touched marched behind the simple mule-drawn wagon that carried his coffin to its burial place. Meanwhile, more than 130 American cities experienced, in Weisbrot's words, "the most concentrated week of

Followed by 50,000 mourners—black and white— a mule-drawn wagon carries the Reverend Martin Luther King, Jr., on his last trip through the streets of Atlanta, Georgia. The wagon and mules were intended to symbolize King's identification with the poor.

racial violence America had ever known." Leaders such as Roy Wilkins used television to plead for calm and denounce the unrest as inappropriate to King's memory, but to the man in the street the violence seemed inevitable, the only possible outlet for his grief.

Fittingly, perhaps, the rioting was worst in Washington, D.C., where, according to one who took part, "everyone participated in the riots. I'm talking about women and children as well as adult males and also young adult males." King's death would prove to be a great tragedy for white society, Stokely Carmichael advised, for he was "the one man of our race that this country's older generations, the militants and the revolutionaries and the masses of black people would still listen to."

*New York City firemen battle
a Harlem storefront blaze,
one of many sparked by Martin
Luther King, Jr.'s assassination
on April 4, 1968. Sending
shockwaves throughout America,
the news of King's death hit
particularly hard in the inner
cities, where grief and rage
took the form of smashed
windows, looted stores,
and burning buildings.*

Carmichael intended his statement as a warning
to white society: that with the death of the apostle of
nonviolence, there was no one who could check the
potentially violent force of black grievance. In retro-
spect, however, his words appear more clearly as a
tragic prediction of the fatal splintering of the black
freedom movement. By the time of King's death,
SNCC and CORE had already purged themselves of
their white members and lost a significant degree
of their former influence. Under the leadership of
Roy Innis, who replaced James Farmer, CORE officially rejected integration as a worthwhile goal for
blacks. In 1968, Carmichael officially merged SNCC
with the Black Panthers. Six months later, Carmichael himself, along with such justly celebrated
veterans of the organization's glory days as Cleveland
Sellers and Willie Ricks, was drummed out of SNCC,
which found itself increasingly confused over tactics

and ideology. By 1969, the organization was all but defunct.

Meanwhile, King's closest friend, the Reverend Ralph Abernathy, had succeeded him as head of SCLC. An admirable figure in many ways, Abernathy possessed few of King's gifts of vision and leadership. Though he was able to carry through King's plans for a Poor People's March on Washington, where in May 1968 several thousand impoverished Americans camped on the mall in tents and crudely fashioned sheds, the protest was hampered by organizational difficulties and regarded with cold indifference by the nation at large. In June police used tear gas to clear the last inhabitants out of Resurrection City (as the encampment was known); bulldozers then plowed the tents and shanties under. Recalling the diastrous 1876 battle between the U.S. cavalry and the Sioux Indians, one participant called it "The Little Bighorn of the civil rights movement."

That same June, Democratic senator Bobby Kennedy, who was regarded by many blacks as their best hope in that year's presidential elections, was assassinated (by a disaffected Jordanian, Sirhan Sirhan) in California. In November, Richard Nixon's election as president seemed to represent the ultimate triumph of the white backlash. As, increasingly, the energy of young white liberals was absorbed by the antiwar movement, Nixon sought to appease white conservatives by stonewalling the implementation of Supreme Court–mandated guidelines for public school integration. (Almost two decades after the *Brown* decision, integrated schools remained the exception in most places in the United States.) Nixon's "Southern Strategy" also included an attempt to appoint an avowed segregationalist, G. Harrold Carswell, to the Supreme Court and opponents accused him of treating the problems of black Americans with what an adviser, Daniel Patrick Moynihan, termed "benign neglect."

The FBI labeled the Black Panthers, who had

In May 1968, six weeks after the death of Martin Luther King, Jr., Resurrection City covers the mall in Washington, D.C. Designed to spotlight SCLC's Poor People's Campaign, the shantytown was wiped out by capital police a month after it opened.

gained a position of influence in certain black urban communities, the single greatest threat to the nation's security, and Nixon's Justice Department established a task force devoted to the party's destruction. In Chicago, police oversaw the assassination of the local chapter's chairman, and by the early 1970s police harassment, ideological wrangling, and the self-destructive behavior of some of the Black Panther leadership had combined to bring about the party's demise.

> **Whether out of hostility, indifference, or exhaustion, it seemed clear that the majority of white Americans, as represented by their federal government, had little more attention to spare for the concerns of their black fellow citizens. The energies of black Americans were far from exhausted; if anything, their history in this country had taught them the futility of despair, the value of perseverance, and the power of hope. Nevertheless, a new generation of black leaders and activists would have to rise to speak for those who had been silenced along the way.**

As the eventful decade of the 1960s drew to a close, one man pronounced himself ready to meet such a challenge. Jesse Jackson, a young minister who had worked with King in Chicago and served as unofficial mayor of Resurrection City, was inspired by his experiences to found a new organization, People United to Save Humanity (PUSH). "When Resurrection City was closed down," Jackson said, "there was a sense of betrayal, a sense of abandonment. The dreamer had been killed in Memphis and there was an attempt now to kill the dream itself, which was to feed the hungry, which was to bring the people together, and rather than come forth with a plan to wipe out

Arrested for leading a court-banned New York City sit-in, the Reverend Jesse Jackson (center) salutes as he heads for jail in February 1971. Later that year, the young Chicago clergyman and former King aide left SCLC to create a new civil rights group, PUSH (People United to Save Humanity): "A new child has been born," proclaimed the charismatic, 30-year-old Jackson.

malnutrition, they were wiping out the malnourished. The first time I had ever really experienced tear gas was in Resurrection City. They drove us out with tear gas. They gassed us. They shot Dr. King. Now they were gassing us. I was determined to keep the struggle moving—if you will, to keep hope alive."

FURTHER READING

Baldwin, James. *The Fire Next Time*. New York: Vintage, 1993.

———. *Nobody Knows My Name*. New York: Vintage, 1993.

———. *Notes of a Native Son*. Boston: Beacon, 1984.

Bennett, Lerone, Jr. *Before the Mayflower: A History of Black America*. 6th ed. New York: Penguin, 1993.

Branch, Taylor. *Parting the Waters: America in the King Years*. New York: Touchstone, 1988.

Brown, Claude. *Manchild in the Promised Land*. New York: New American Library, 1965.

Carson, Clayborne. *In Struggle: SNCC and the Black Awakening of the 1960s*. Cambridge: Harvard University Press, 1981.

Carson, Clayborne, et al., eds. *The Eyes on the Prize Civil Rights Reader: Documents, Speeches, and Firsthand Accounts from the Black Freedom Struggle, 1954–1990*. New York: Penguin, 1991.

Cleaver, Eldridge. *Soul on Ice*. New York: Dell, 1992.

Franklin, John Hope. *From Slavery to Freedom: A History of Negro Americans*. New York: Penguin, 1988.

Garrow, David J. *Bearing the Cross: Martin Luther King and the Southern Christian Leadership Conference*. New York: Vintage, 1988.

Grant, Joanne, ed. *Black Protest: History, Documents, and Analyses*. New York: Ballantine, 1991.

Hampton, Henry, and Steve Fayer. *Voices of Freedom: An Oral History of the Civil Rights Struggle from the 1950s Through the 1980s*. New York: Bantam, 1990.

Leuchtenberg, William. *A Troubled Feast: American Society Since 1945*. Boston: Little, Brown, 1979.

Malcolm X, with Alex Haley. *The Autobiography of Malcolm X*. New York: Grove Press, 1965.

Weisbrot, Robert. *Freedom Bound: A History of America's Civil Rights Movement*. New York: Plume, 1991.

Wittner, Lawrence. *Cold War America: From Hiroshima to Watergate*. New York: Holt Rinehart, 1978.

INDEX

Abernathy, Ralph, 55, 137
Ali, Muhammad, 121, 127–34
Armstrong, Louis, 90

Baldwin, James, 27, 64–66, 72, 74, 81, 90, 96
Basie, William "Count," 85, 90
Bearing the Cross: Martin Luther King and the Southern Christian Leadership Conference (Garrow), 30
Bennett, Lerone, 74
Bevel, James, 36, 38
Birmingham, Alabama, 28, 29, 31, 34, 88
Black Panther Party, 118, 136, 137, 138
"Black Power," 80–83, 126, 129
Bloody Sunday, 41, 45, 47
Bond, Julian, 93
Boynton, Amelia, 27, 33, 40
Brooke, Edward, 76
Brown, H. Rap, 83, 118
Brown v. Board of Education of Topeka, Kansas, 23, 26, 137

Carmichael, Stokely, 50, 51, 78, 80, 81, 83, 111, 118, 135, 136
Chaney, James, 47
Charles, Ray, 86, 87, 96
Chicago, Illinois, 69, 88, 113, 138
    riots, 63, 73, 76
Civil Rights Acts
    1957, 17
    1964, 17, 29
Clark, Jim, 14, 27, 31, 32, 33, 34, 36, 37, 38, 40, 43, 45, 52, 54
Congress, U.S., 29, 41, 55, 59, 114, 115
Congress of Racial Equality (CORE), 24, 44, 47, 74, 79, 80, 136
Connor, "Bull," 28, 112
Cooper, Annie Lee, 34
Cosby, Bill, 97

Davis, Miles, 98, 99–101
Deacons for Defense, 80
Dennis, Dave, 47
Detroit, Michigan, 59, 70–72, 85, 88
    riots, 63, 70
"Down at the Cross" (Baldwin), 64–66

Ellington, Duke, 90, 91
Ellison, Ralph, 96
Evers, Medgar, 25

Farmer, James, 44, 74, 136
Federal Bureau of Investigation (FBI), 27, 52, 131, 137
"Fifth Avenue, Uptown" (Baldwin), 74
Fire Next Time, The (Baldwin), 65
Forman, James, 27, 44, 45, 52, 53, 64
Franklin, Aretha, 85–89, 96, 134
Franklin, John Hope, 74
Freedom Bound: A History of America's Civil Rights Movement (Weisbrot), 19, 60
Freedom rides, 44
Frye, Marquette, 60
Frye, Ronald, 60

Giovanni, Nikki, 89
"Great Society," 63, 66, 110
Greensboro sit-ins, 75

Hendrix, Jimi, 101–03
Holiday, Billie, 85, 86, 90, 91
Hulett, John, 78

Innis, Roy, 136
In Struggle (Carson), 50

Jackson, Jesse, 138–39
Jackson, Jimmie Lee, 38, 106
Jackson, Mahalia, 88
Jersey City, New Jersey, riots, 62
Johnson, Lyndon B., 17, 30, 36, 50, 51, 53, 54, 59, 63, 67, 71, 76, 105, 108, 109, 111

Kennedy, John F., 20, 25
King, Coretta Scott, 50
King, Martin Luther, Jr., 24, 43, 44, 45, 46, 50, 53, 64, 80, 81, 88, 89, 119, 133, 137, 138
    assassination, 134–35, 138, 139
    F. B. I, campaign against, 52, 111
    and housing discrimination, 67–69, 78, 114
    March on Washington, 49
    Montgomery bus boycott, 21–22
    Nobel Peace Prize, 28, 36, 49
    Selma protest, 27, 29–38, 68
    Selma-to-Montgomery march, 38–44, 55–57, 59
    and Vietnam War, 105, 108–11, 113, 114, 118
Ku Klux Klan, 59

Lafayette, Bernard, 26
Lawson, James, 45

Lee, George, 23
Levison, Stanley, 68, 69
Lewis, John, 15, 16, 27, 30, 32, 33, 39, 40, 45, 52, 55, 78, 80, 111
Literacy tests, 18, 30
Lowndes County Freedom Organization, 78, 118

Malcolm X, 48–50, 64, 80, 119, 128, 133
Manchild in the Promised Land (Brown), 71–72
"March Against Fear," 79
March on Washington, 49
Meredith, James, 79
Monk, Thelonious, 91
Montgomery bus boycott, 21–22, 23, 67
Moses, Bob, 22, 24, 25, 45, 46, 47, 105–7
Music, 85–103

National Association for the Advancement of Colored People (NAACP), 24, 25, 26, 76, 80, 105, 111
National Urban League, 67, 70, 80, 105, 111
Nation of Islam, 48, 49, 50, 64, 126, 128
Newark, New Jersey, riots, 63, 75
New York City, 64, 67, 74, 88, 110, 133
    riots, 63, 76
Nixon, Richard, 77, 118, 137, 138

Parker, Charlie "Bird," 91
Parting the Waters (Branch), 88
Patterson, New Jersey, riots, 62
People United to Save Humanity (PUSH), 90, 138
Poll tax, 19
Poor People's March on Washington, 137
Presley, Elvis, 93, 94

Reeb, James, 106
Reese, Frederick, 47
Resurrection City, 137, 138, 139
Ricks, Willie, 136
Rowan, Carl, 111
Rustin, Bayard, 64

Segregation, 17, 28, 67, 68, 128
    in housing, 67, 69, 114
    in public education, 17, 23, 56, 77, 137
    on public transportation, 21–22, 23, 44, 56
Sellers, Cleveland, 136
Selma demonstrations, 13–17, 26–38, 48, 50, 51, 52, 67, 68, 78
Selma-to-Montgomery march, 38–44, 55–57, 90
Shuttlesworth, Fred, 47, 48
Southern Christian Leadership Conference (SCLC), 15, 17, 24, 26, 27, 28, 29, 30,

31, 33, 36, 37, 38, 43,
47, 78, 79, 80, 88, 105,
137
Sports, 121–34
Stokes, Carl, 114
Student Nonviolent Coor-
dinating Committee
(SNCC), 15, 16, 17,
22, 24, 26, 27, 28,
29, 30, 31, 41, 43, 46,
47, 48, 49, 50, 52, 75,
78, 79, 80, 93, 105,
107, 108, 111, 118,
136
Supreme Court, U.S., 23,
133, 137

Till, Emmett, 22, 23
"Tuesday Turnaround,"
43, 45, 49

Vietnam War, 36, 77,
103, 105–14, 121, 126,
131, 133
Vivian, C. T., 37, 52,
54
Voices of Freedom (Fayer
and Hampton), 24, 34,
47, 78, 111
Voting rights, 17–20, 23,
26–44, 55–57, 59
Voting Rights Act of
1965, 55, 59–60, 93

Wallace, George, 38, 77
War on Poverty, 71, 110, 114
Washington, D.C., riots, 135
Watts, Los Angeles, 70, 72
riots, 60–62, 63, 69, 74–75
White Citizens Council
(WCC), 26
Wilkins, Roy, 76, 111, 118,
135
Williams, Hosea, 15, 16, 39,
40
Wright, Mose, 22, 23

Young, Andrew, 24, 33
Young, Whitney, 111, 118
Younge, Sammy, 107

PICTURE CREDITS

SEAN DOLAN has a degree in literature and American history from the State University of New York. He is the author of many biographies and histories for young adult readers.

CLAYBORNE CARSON, senior consulting editor of the MILESTONES IN BLACK AMERICAN HISTORY series, is a professor of history at Stanford University. His first book, *In Struggle: SNCC and the Black Awakening of the 1960s* (1981), won the Frederick Jackson Turner Prize of the Organization of American Historians. He is the director of the Martin Luther King, Jr., Papers Project, which will publish 12 volumes of King's writings.

DARLENE CLARK HINE, senior consulting editor of the MILESTONES IN BLACK AMERICAN HISTORY series, is the John A. Hannah Professor of American History at Michigan State University. She is the author of numerous books and articles on black women's history. Her most recent work is the two-volume *Black Women in America: An Historical Encyclopedia* (1993).